W9-BHT-175

FOUNDATIONS
in PERSONAL
FINANCE®

DAVE RAMSEY

It is unlawful to copy or reproduce any part of the student workbook without the written consent of the publisher.

LAMPO
PRESS

Copyright © 2008 by Lampo Licensing LLC

Notice of Rights

All rights reserved. No part of this publication may be reproduced or transmitted in any form or by any means, electronic or mechanical, including photocopy, recording, or any information storage and retrieval system, without written permission from the publisher.

Permissions

Requests for permission to make copies of any part of the work should be mailed to:

Permissions—Curriculum Department
The Lampo Group, Inc.
1749 Mallory Lane, Suite 100
Brentwood, TN 37027

Note to the Reader

This publication is designed to provide accurate and authoritative information with regard to the subject matter covered. It is sold with the understanding that the publisher is not engaged in rendering financial, accounting, or other professional advice. If financial advice or other expert professional assistance is required, the services of a competent professional person should be sought.

4 5 6 7 8 9 10   11 11 10

Printed and bound in the United States of America

ISBN 978-0-9816839-6-6

ACKNOWLEDGEMENTS

The Lampo Group, Inc. would like to give special thanks to the following educators for their assistance with this project. Their input was essential for creating a financial literacy curriculum that meets the needs of the students and empowers them in the area of personal finance.

Jean Ambrose
Family and Consumer Science Teacher
Hall-Dale High School
Farmingdale, Maine

Major Richard Bensemon
Senior Aerospace Science Instructor
Northridge AFJROTC UT-931
Layton, Utah

Jan Christmas
Spanish, Government, Economics and
Art History Teacher
Henry T. Waskow High School
Belton, Texas

Lindsey Chunn
Resource Management Teacher
Olive Branch High School
Olive Branch, Mississippi

Matthew Daniel
Economics Teacher
Cannon County High School
Woodbury, Tennessee

Jerry L. Dent
LEAP Alternative Education Instructor
Lakeview High School
Lakeview, Michigan

Kent Eberspacher
Business Teacher
Star Valley High School
Afton, Wyoming

Allen Harris
Director of Content Development
Dave Ramsey's Financial Peace University
Nashville, Tennessee

Kathy L. Jarman
Business and English Teacher
Helias High School
Jefferson City, Missouri

Penny Kugler
Assistant Professor of Economics
Director, Center for Economic Education
University of Central Missouri
Warrensburg, Missouri

Sherri McAfee
Business Teacher
Elida High School
Elida, New Mexico

Len McKnatt
Economics Teacher
Battle Ground Academy
Franklin, Tennessee

Kregg Parenti
Computer and Personal Finance Teacher
Berean Christian School
West Palm Beach, Florida

Jeff Rogers
Work-Based Learning Coordinator
Heritage High School
Conyers, Georgia

Cathy M. Taylor
Math Teacher
Satsuma High School
Satsuma, Alabama

Terri Winkle
Business Teacher
Western Heights High School
Oklahoma City, Oklahoma

Curriculum Development
Brenda Thompson

Editing
Mark Ballinger
Daniel Chunn
Grace Clausing
Rachel DeMass
Joe Finlay
Lindsey Foster
Allen Harris
Chris Huovinen
Marcie Kindred
Jim King
Kim Little
Jason Lowrey
Jason Mayes
Chris Russell
Richard Speight
Jane Storie
Beth Tallent
David Taylor
Matt Woodburn

Creative Direction
Paul Farmer
Brian Williams

Design and Animation
Josh Hancock
Jeff Hunter
Ken Pruiksma

Video Production
Carl Diebold, Sincera Video

Dave Ramsey, a personal money management expert, is an extremely popular national radio personality, and author of the *New York Times* best-sellers *The Total Money Makeover, Financial Peace* and *More Than Enough*. Ramsey added television host to his title in 2007 when "The Dave Ramsey Show on the Fox Business Network" debuted nationally. Ramsey knows first-hand what financial peace means in his own life—living a true rags-to-riches-to-rags-to-riches story. By age twenty-six he had established a four-million-dollar real estate portfolio, only to lose it by age thirty. He has since rebuilt his financial life and now devotes himself full-time to helping ordinary people understand the forces behind their financial distress and how to set things right. He resides with his wife Sharon and their three children in Nashville, Tennessee.

As Dave Ramsey's kid, **Rachel Ramsey** knows a thing or two about money. From an early age, Rachel's parents instilled in her a healthy sense of financial responsibility. She learned the value of earning, saving and giving—and how debt is the enemy of wealth. Armed with this valuable knowledge, Rachel desires to help others—especially teens and college students—understand the importance of money management. An experienced public speaker, Rachel often joins her father on stage in capacity-crowd arenas to teach basic financial literacy skills. Now in college, Rachel successfully manages her own finances while majoring in Communication Studies.

TABLE OF CONTENTS

A LETTER FROM DAVE

Dear Student,

Welcome to Foundations in Personal Finance! The information you are about to learn will change your financial future—if you apply what we teach.

I talk to people every day who tell me, "I wish I had learned this stuff in high school! I could have avoided so many problems!"

I know how they feel. I built a multi-million-dollar business in my twenties, only to have it wiped out because I didn't know how to manage my money—and I even had a college finance degree!

You don't want to learn about money the hard way like I did. If you take what you learn from this class and apply it to your life, you'll never have to experience the pain and stress money problems can bring.

Our friends at Fifth Third Bank understand what a difference it makes when people know how to manage their money. That's why they're sponsoring Foundations in Personal Finance in your school. We appreciate Fifth Third Bank for their support in bringing this class to you. They're helping you become a generation of future millionaires!

Enjoy the class! Use what you learn! Change your life!

Sincerely,

UNIT 1
SAVING and INVESTING

What do other high school students know about saving?

We asked high school students to describe something they really wanted and thought they *had* to buy, only to realize later that they wasted their money.

" I worked and saved **$250** for a guitar that I **never learned how to play.** "

Junior, Michigan

"I bought some fish that I thought I really wanted. I never fed them, totally lost interest in them, and they all died. What a waste of money."

Junior, Alabama

"I really wanted this expensive skateboard that cost $130. I had to have it. Turned out it skated no better than the other ones that were a lot less expensive."

Sophomore, Alabama

"I bought a computer game that didn't work because I didn't read the required hardware notice on the box."

Senior, Missouri

"I got a pink Coach purse that I paid over $200 for and have maybe used twice."

Junior, Florida

LEARNING OUTCOMES

List the Baby Steps.

Explain the three basic reasons for saving money.

Identify the benefits of having an emergency fund.

Demonstrate how compound interest works and understand the impact of annual interest rate.

KEY TERMS

Baby Steps
Compound Interest
Emergency Fund
Interest Rate
Money Market
Sinking Fund

BEFORE YOU BEGIN

What do you know about saving?

Before watching the lesson, read each statement below and mark whether you agree or disagree in the "before" column. Then, after watching the lesson, do it again using the "after" column to see if you changed your mind on any question.

Before				After	
Agree	Disagree			Agree	Disagree
☐	☐	1. The amount of money you save depends on how much money you earn. Simply put, you will *save* more when you *earn* more.		☐	☐
☐	☐	2. A savings account at your bank is the best place to put your emergency fund.		☐	☐
☐	☐	3. The two biggest factors in compound interest and building wealth are time and the initial amount of the investment.		☐	☐
☐	☐	4. It is okay to use your emergency fund to pay cash for big purchases such as a TV or a cell phone.		☐	☐
☐	☐	5. You should pay yourself first before you pay bills.		☐	☐

What are your initial thoughts about saving?

....

....

....

....

....

....

What do you want to learn about saving?

....

....

....

....

....

....

The Seven Baby Steps

Step 1
$1,000 in an emergency fund (or $500 if you make less than $20,000 a year)

Step 2
Pay off all debt except the house utilizing the debt snowball

Step 3
Three to six months expenses in savings

Step 4
Invest 15% of your household income into Roth IRAs and pre-tax retirement plans

Step 5
College funding

Step 6
Pay off your home early

Step 7
Build wealth and give!

MORE INFO

The **Seven Baby Steps** are the steps you should take to reach financial peace.

If you are not in debt, these steps will serve as your compass or framework for financial success.

You will find the Seven Baby Steps explained in detail throughout this course. When you begin implementing them for yourself, be sure to follow them in order and complete each one before moving on to the next.

MONEY FACTS

70% of consumers live paycheck to paycheck.
The Wall Street Journal

The United States has a **-.6%** savings rate.
Department of Commerce

Only **41%** of Americans save regularly.
Federal Reserve System

Half of American households live on less than $46,326 a year.
U.S. Census Bureau

REAL LIFE

Do you think people who *make* more actually *save* more? Think again. Harris Interactive conducted a survey for CareerBuilder. com (November/ December 2006) of 6,169 full time adult workers. The survey, according to a Reuters news release, found that 19% of workers who make over $100,000 live paycheck to paycheck.

Take the First Step

 Baby Step 1 is _____ in an emergency fund.

If you make under $20,000 a year, put _____ in an emergency fund.

_____ must become a priority. Always pay _____ first.

The United States has a _____ savings rate.

Saving money is about _____ and _____.

Money is _____.   **END OF VIDEO PART 1**

You should save money for three basic reasons:

1. _____
2. _____
3. _____

Emergency Fund

_____ are going to happen. Count on it.

Baby Step 1, a beginner emergency fund, is _____ in the bank (or $500 if your household income is below $20,000 per year).

Baby Step 3 is a fully funded emergency fund of 3-6 months of expenses.

A great place to keep your emergency fund is in a _____ _____ account from a mutual fund company.

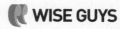 **WISE GUYS**

"If you do the things you need to do when you need to do them, then someday you can do the things you want to do when you want to do them."

Zig Ziglar

"I'm 14 and want to buy a car in a couple of years. How much money will it take to get a good one?"

DAVE'S ANSWER: You can buy a good used car for around $3,000. This may seem like a lot right now, but let me show you how easy it can be. Let's say you work part-time after school and on weekends. If you make $100 a week and save it all, you'll have enough for a car in only eight months. Pretty cool, huh?

Can't do $100 a week? Saving a little bit at a time adds up and you will eventually reach your goal. Take a look at the graph below for a few ways it can be done.

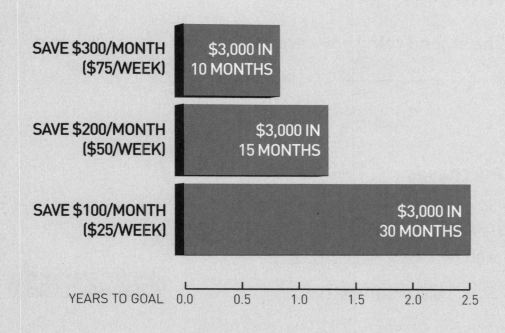

SAVE $300/MONTH ($75/WEEK): $3,000 IN 10 MONTHS

SAVE $200/MONTH ($50/WEEK): $3,000 IN 15 MONTHS

SAVE $100/MONTH ($25/WEEK): $3,000 IN 30 MONTHS

YEARS TO GOAL 0.0 0.5 1.0 1.5 2.0 2.5

"How should I prepare to manage my money when I go off to college and what should I do when I'm there?"

DAVE'S ANSWER: One thing you want to be sure to do in college is avoid credit cards. They're going to be tempting you on every corner. And of course, you need to learn how to operate, balance and reconcile a checkbook.

You also need to learn how to do a zero-based budget where you look at what you're going to spend every month. A friend of mine gives his college-age daughter $200 a month for expenses and she has to do a written plan showing exactly what she's going to do with that money before each month begins.

MORE INFO

For example...

Say you borrow $4,000 to purchase a dining room set.

Most furniture stores will sell their financing contracts to finance companies.

This means you will have borrowed at 24% with payments of $211 per month for 24 months. So, you will pay a total of $5,064, plus insurance, for that set.

But if you save the same $211 per month for only 18 months, you will be able to pay cash.

When you pay cash, you can almost always negotiate a discount, so you will be able to buy it even earlier.

Your emergency fund is not an _____, it is insurance.

Do not _____ this fund for purchases.

The emergency fund is your _____ savings priority. Do it quickly!

The second thing you save money for is _____.

Purchases

Instead of _____ to purchase, pay cash by using a _____ _____ approach.

END OF VIDEO PART 2

Wealth Building

The third thing you save money for is

_____ _____.

_____ is a key ingredient when it comes to wealth building.

Building wealth is a _____, not a sprint.

Pre-_____ _____(PACs) withdrawals are a good way to build in discipline.

_____ _____ is a mathematical explosion. You must start _____.

MORE INFO

You should have an emergency fund because unexpected things are going to happen. Smart people have known this for centuries and used to say, "In the house of the wise are stores of choice food and oil, but a foolish man devours all he has." (Proverbs 21:20) In other words, having some money saved back can turn a crisis into an inconvenience.

Compound Interest Is Powerful

Take a one-time investment of $1,000 and earn 10% on it. Your interest at the end of the year is $100. Add that to your original $1,000 and you have $1,100. At the end of the next year, your $1,100 is compounded at 10% interest, so your return on investment is $110. Add that to the $1,100 and you now have $1,210. Your interest on $1,210 is $121. So as time passes, the amount you earn from interest grows. That is why it is so important that you start now. You have more time for your interest to snowball and pick up more and more snow!

How to Calculate Compound Interest

Use this simple formula to figure out the future value of a deposit once compound interest has worked its magic.

$$FV = PV(1+r/m)^{mt}$$

When calculating this formula, remember to use the mathematical order of operations.

FV is the future value
PV is the present value
r is the annual rate of interest as a decimal (5% is expressed as the decimal .05)
m is the number of times per year the interest is compounded (monthly, annually, etc.)
t is the number of years you leave it invested

REAL LIFE

Compound interest is interest paid on interest previously earned; credited daily, monthly, quarterly, semi-annually, or annually on both principal and previously credited interest.

! STUPID TAX

"I played this internet game site where you could buy extra 'pixel' clothing and hairstyles.
I ended up spending over $100 on pixels for the game."

Freshman, Alabama

"I blew all my money trying to get a stuffed animal out of one of those machines with the claws."

Junior, Florida

💬 FEEDBACK

"I've read some of Dave Ramsey's stuff and learned a ton. As soon as I turned 16, I started working and have been saving money ever since. After just over a year of working, I have saved between $5,000–$6,000 to buy a car. What he says really works."

Senior, Alabama

The Story of Ben and Arthur

Both save $2,000 per year at 12%. Ben starts at age 19 and stops at age 26, while Arthur starts at age 27 and stops at age 65.

END OF VIDEO PART 3

Saving only $167 a month!

AGE	BEN INVESTS:		ARTHUR INVESTS:	
19	2,000	2,240	0	0
20	2,000	4,749	0	0
21	2,000	7,558	0	0
22	2,000	10,706	0	0
23	2,000	14,230	0	0
24	2,000	18,178	0	0
25	2,000	22,599	0	0
26	2,000	27,551	0	0
27	0	30,857	2,000	2,240
28	0	34,560	2,000	4,749
29	0	38,708	2,000	7,558
30	0	43,352	2,000	10,706
31	0	48,554	2,000	14,230
32	0	54,381	2,000	18,178
33	0	60,907	2,000	22,599
34	0	68,216	2,000	27,551
35	0	76,802	2,000	33,097
36	0	85,570	2,000	39,309
37	0	95,383	2,000	46,266
38	0	107,339	2,000	54,058
39	0	120,220	2,000	62,785
40	0	134,646	2,000	72,559
41	0	150,804	2,000	83,506
42	0	168,900	2,000	95,767
43	0	189,168	2,000	109,499
44	0	211,869	2,000	124,879
45	0	237,293	2,000	142,104
46	0	265,768	2,000	161,396
47	0	297,660	2,000	183,004
48	0	333,379	2,000	207,204
49	0	373,385	2,000	234,308
50	0	418,191	2,000	264,665
51	0	468,374	2,000	298,665
52	0	524,579	2,000	336,745
53	0	587,528	2,000	379,394
54	0	658,032	2,000	427,161
55	0	736,995	2,000	480,660
56	0	825,435	2,000	540,579
57	0	924,487	2,000	607,688
58	0	1,035,425	2,000	682,851
59	0	1,159,676	2,000	767,033
60	0	1,298,837	2,000	861,317
61	0	1,454,698	2,000	966,915
62	0	1,629,261	2,000	1,085,185
63	0	1,824,773	2,000	1,217,647
64	0	2,043,746	2,000	1,366,005
65	0	**2,288,996**	2,000	**1,532,166**

Arthur invested $78,000 and NEVER caught up!

Ben invested only $16,000!

Rate of Return, or _____ rate, is important.

◀ END OF VIDEO PART 4

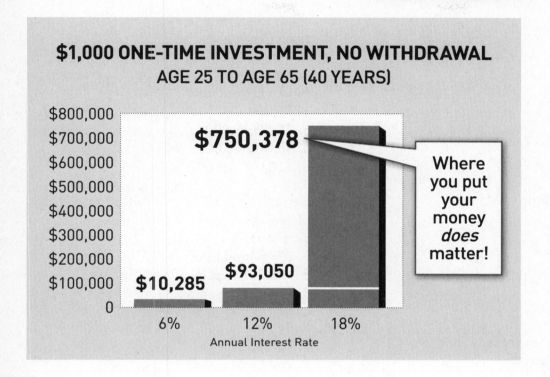

$1,000 ONE-TIME INVESTMENT, NO WITHDRAWAL
AGE 25 TO AGE 65 (40 YEARS)

$750,378

Where you put your money *does* matter!

$10,285 — 6%
$93,050 — 12%
18%

Annual Interest Rate

💲 MONEY FACTS

81% of teens agree "it's important to me to have a lot of money in my life."
Charles Schwab survey

Only **22%** of teens say they know how to invest money to make it grow.
Charles Schwab survey

84% of teens have some money saved, with an average of $1,044.
Charles Schwab survey

1 in 4 (24%) teens agree that since they are young, saving money isn't that important.
Charles Schwab survey

Recap and Review

Make savings a priority. START NOW!

Compound interest works over time and the rate of return will make a difference in how large your investment grows. Remember Ben and Arthur.

An emergency fund is your backup strategy when unexpected financial events happen. Baby Step 1 is $1,000 in your emergency fund ($500 if you earn less than $20,000).

Discipline and focused emotion is the key to saving.

Use the 80/20 rule. Handling money is 80% behavior and only 20% head knowledge. Anyone can learn to save!

Vocabulary

Amoral
Baby Steps
Compound Interest
Emergency Fund
Interest Rate
Money Market
Murphy's Law
Pre-Authorized Checking
Priority
Sinking Fund

Matching

a. money market
b. $500/$1,000 in an emergency fund
c. 3-6 months of expenses
d. pay off debt
e. amoral
f. discipline
g. compound interest
h. Murphy's Law
i. sinking fund
j. savings account

___ 1. Saving money for a purchase and letting the interest work for you rather than against you

___ 2. Money is neither good nor bad

___ 3. Emergency Fund goes here

___ 4. Interest on interest

___ 5. If it can go wrong, it will; unexpected events

___ 6. Baby Step 1

___ 7. Baby Step 3

___ 8. Key to wealth building

Multiple Choice

9. For most people, a fully-funded emergency fund will be about:
   a. $1,000
   b. $3,000-5,000
   c. $5,000-10,000
   d. $10,000-15,000

10. Ben and Arthur illustrate which principle of saving?
    a. rule of 72
    b. compound interest
    c. simple interest
    d. none of the above

11. Baby Steps 1 and 3 have to do with:
    a. saving
    b. emergency fund
    c. getting out of debt
    d. both a and b

12. You should save for the following:
    a. emergency fund
    b. purchases
    c. wealth building
    d. all of the above

13. How many Baby Steps are there?
    a. 4
    b. 5
    c. 6
    d. 7

14. Saving is about contentment and:
    a. emotion
    b. greed
    c. having money
    d. pride

15. The following is true about PACs:
    a. stands for Personal Account Coordinator
    b. stands for Pre-Authorized Checking
    c. helps build discipline when saving
    d. both b and c

16. The saving habits of Ben and Arthur help to illustrate the principal of compound interest.
    a. true
    b. false

17. Dave's 80/20 rule says when it comes to money, 80% is head knowledge and 20% is behavior.
    a. true
    b. false

18. Your income level greatly affects your savings habits.
    a. true
    b. false

19. Interest is money paid to a saver by a financial institution.
    a. true
    b. false

20. The correct order for using your money is: pay bills, save, then give.
    a. true
    b. false

Short Answer

21. Why do you think the United States has a negative savings rate? How does this relate to your personal savings habits?

22. List the Baby Steps. Why do you think Dave skips Baby Step 2 in this lesson?

23. Explain the relationship between having an emergency fund and Murphy's Law.

24. Calculate the compound interest for each problem below:
    • $1,000 at 6% interest for three years
    • $500 at 18% interest for four years
    • $1,500 at 12% interest for two years

25. What are the three primary savings goals?

26. What changes can you make now in your own life based on what you saw in the video? How will these changes help?

27. Why do you need an emergency fund at your age?

28. Why do you need to have $1,000 in the bank before paying off debt?

29. How does compound interest differ from simple interest?

Case Studies

30. What was the most important piece of information or concept you learned from this lesson? How will you apply it to your life?

31. Jeremy has been out of school for two years, has a good job, and recently got a raise. He is excited about investing and always puts part of his check into savings. Although he has $6,500 in debt left to pay, he is making more than the minimum payments and should be debt free in 15 months. Should he continue to save or pay off his debts? Justify your answer.

32. Melissa is about to get a $200 per month raise. She wants a new television and some furniture. She has $500 in her savings account and figures with her raise she will have the cash to make her purchases easily within a few months. She also has $1,000 in available credit remaining on her credit card and is thinking about using it to buy everything now rather than waiting until she has the money. What would you tell Melissa? Justify your answer.

INVESTMENT OPTIONS  CH 2

What do other high school students know about investing?

We asked high school students to describe the weirdest get rich quick scheme they've ever heard of.

> "Someone told me that I could **get rich selling food** door to door. After three days of **embarrassment**, I ended up **only $5 richer**."
>
> Junior, Michigan

"I know about a chain letter where you put $1 in an envelope, include six addresses and send it out to the top address. Eventually people are supposed to send you $1 each."

Junior, Alabama

"I've heard people say you can go to Alaska and work in a canning plant to get rich."

Senior, Wyoming

"People think you can go to Hollywood and become a street performer until a big-time producer discovers you and you become a rich actor."

Junior, Missouri

"Someone told me to hide my money where I would forget about it and wouldn't spend it."

Senior, Tennessee

LEARNING OUTCOMES

Explain the KISS rule of investing.

Examine the relationship between diversification and risk.

Compare and contrast different types of investments: money markets, bonds, single stocks, mutual funds, rental real estate, and annuities.

KEY TERMS

Diversification
Liquidity
Mutual Fund
Risk
Risk Return Ratio
Share

What do you know about investing?

Before watching the lesson, read each statement below and mark whether you agree or disagree in the "before" column. Then, after watching the lesson, do it again using the "after" column to see if you changed your mind on any question.

Before			After	
Agree	Disagree		Agree	Disagree
☐	☐	1. A mutual fund is a collection of money from different investors used to purchase stocks, bonds, and so on, and is managed by a fund manager.	☐	☐
☐	☐	2. Investing is for a minimum of three years— less than that is savings.	☐	☐
☐	☐	3. The more sophisticated the investment, the more money you get in return.	☐	☐
☐	☐	4. With virtually all investments, as the risk goes up, so does the potential return.	☐	☐
☐	☐	5. It's hard to find an investment that will average 12% for 10 years or more.	☐	☐

List your initial thoughts about investing.

What do you want to learn about investing?

KISS Rule of Investing

Keep it _____, _____!

Never invest purely for _____ _____.

Never invest using _____ money.

Diversification

_____ means to spread around.

Diversification _____ risk. ◀ **END OF VIDEO PART 1**

💲 MONEY FACTS

$12,356 trillion— the combined assets of the Investment Company Institute's 8,015 mutual funds as of October 2007.

Investment Company Institute

51% of teens report that their main reason for saving is to have enough money for long-term future plans, like college or a car.

Charles Schwab Survey

12% of teens have stocks and investments in an account that is held in their name.

Charles Schwab Survey

The Power of Diversification

What would happen if two people each invested $10,000—one diversifies, the other does not—and left it alone for 25 years?

Investor 1 invests... $10,000 for 25 years at 7%

Investor 2 invests...
$2,000 and loses it all
$2,000 under his mattress
$2,000 at 5% return
$2,000 at 10% return
$2,000 at 15% return

Investor 2: Over $116,000 because of diversification!

Investor 1: Just $57,254 without diversification!

$120k
$110k
$100k
$90k
$80k
$70k
$60k
$50k
$40k
$30k
$20k
$10k
$0k

A difference of almost $59,000!

➕ MORE INFO

Throughout the stock market's history:
▶ 97% of five-year periods made money
▶ 100% of 10-year periods made money.

MORE INFO

The Securities Exchange Commission (SEC) is the government agency responsible for regulating the stock market. It was created in 1934 to increase public trust after the 1929 stock market crash and the years of the Great Depression.

Risk Return Ratio and Liquidity

With virtually all investments, as the _____ goes up, so does the potential return.

When discussing investments, _____ is availability.

As there is more liquidity, there is typically _____ return.

END OF VIDEO PART 2

Types of Investments

1. Money Markets

A C.D. is a _____ ___ _____, typically at a bank.

"I am 19 years old and working in my family's business. I live at home with my parents and my car is completely paid for. How should I start saving for a house and retirement? I want to make sure I am doing everything I can to avoid financial problems in the future. What do I need to do?"

DAVE'S ANSWER: Your first goal should be to save 3-6 months of your income (since you don't really have any expenses). This will be your full emergency fund. Then you should save for anything you plan on doing in the next few years, like getting married or buying a home.

On top of that, you should invest into a Roth IRA. The contribution limit for 2008 is $5,000 per year, which comes out to about $416 per month. You can do less than that, but not more. If you start that now, you will be extremely wealthy when you retire.

Money market mutual funds are _____risk money market accounts with check writing privileges. These are great for _____ _____.

2. Single Stocks

Single stock investing carries an extremely _____ degree of risk.

When you buy stock, you are buying a small piece of _____ in the company.

Your return comes as the company increases in _____ or pays you, its owner, some of the profits (_____).

3. Bonds

A bond is a _____ instrument by which the company owes _____ money.

Your return is the fluctuation in price and the _____ rate paid. Few individuals do well with _____ _____ purchases. **END OF VIDEO PART 3**

4. Mutual Funds

Investors pool their _____ to invest.

Portfolio managers manage the pool or _____.

Your _____ comes as the _____ of the fund is increased. **END OF VIDEO PART 4**

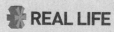 **REAL LIFE**

Harry, a bright young man, was fresh out of college when Bob approached him with an investment opportunity that sounded too good to pass up.

"I've got some property on a potential oil field," Bob said. "For only $750 you can buy a share of the land. You'd be crazy not to get in on this investment." Bob, an expert salesman, promised Harry would become rich, and sealed the deal with a simple appeal: "Harry, this is a great way to diversify your portfolio."

Thirty years later, after all the oil was pumped out, Harry still hadn't seen any money from his "investment." It turns out that Bob was offering rights to land that he didn't have the right to sell, scamming people by selling "phantom shares." Harry's risky attempt to diversify cost him $750.

What would have happened if he put that money in a mutual fund at 12% interest instead? He would now have $22,469.

Mutual funds that are properly diversified will have investment dollars spread equally among four different classes of financial assets.

- 25% International
- 25% Aggressive Growth (Small Cap)
- 25% Growth (Mid Cap)
- 25% Growth and Income (Large Cap)

Mutual funds are good _____ term investments.

> **END OF VIDEO PART 5**

5. Real Estate

Least _____ consumer investment.

You should have lots of _____ before using real estate as an _____.

6. Annuities

Annuities are _____ accounts with an _____ company.

_____ annuities are at a low interest rate of around 5%, aren't really fixed, and are a _____ investment.

_____ annuities are mutual funds sheltered by the annuity covering, thereby allowing the mutual fund to grow tax-deferred.

WISE GUYS

"October. This is one of the peculiarly dangerous months to speculate in stocks. The others are July, January, September, April, November, May, March, June, December, August, and February."

Mark Twain

Horrible Investments

Gold

_____ & Futures

Day _____

Viaticals

> **END OF VIDEO PART 6**

"I'm 21 and currently in college. Next month, I'll be receiving an inheritance of about $40,000. I don't know anything about stocks, mutual funds or C.D.s, but I don't want to lose all this money. I don't have any debt, so what should I do?"

DAVE'S ANSWER: I'm glad you're asking questions. One of the fastest ways to lose money is to put it into an investment that you don't understand.

You don't need to change your major to Finance to make this happen, but you do have a $40,000 responsibility that you didn't have before. For now, a simple savings account is fine. I'd park $30,000 in there and just forget about it for a while. Then use $5,000 to set up an emergency fund and maybe blow $5,000 on some things just for you. After all, spending and having fun with money is still important!

But here's something to think about once you've educated yourself on investing. If you put that remaining $30,000 in a good growth stock mutual fund, by the time you're ready to retire you'll be looking at about $10 million.

Talk about being able to retire with dignity and change your family tree!

Recap and Review

Start investing now.

Diversify. Don't put your money in only one place. Spreading out your money lowers your risk.

NEVER put money into something that you don't understand. If you do not understand an investment well enough to teach someone else how it works, don't buy it.

Building wealth takes time. It is not like a microwave; it's like a crock pot.

 MORE INFO

Growth and income funds are very stable and known as large-cap funds.

Growth funds are sometimes known as mid-cap funds and are still growing.

Aggressive growth funds are wilder and known as small-cap funds.

Vocabulary

Aggressive Growth Stock Mutual Fund
Annuity
Bond
C.D.
Commodity
Diversification
Dividend
Fixed Annuity
Futures
Investments
Growth Stock Mutual Fund
Large-Cap Fund
Liquidity
Mid-Cap Fund
Money Market
Mutual Fund
Portfolio
Rental Real Estate
Risk
International Stock Mutual Fund
Risk Return Ratio
Savings Account
Share
Single Stocks
Small-Cap Fund
Speculative
Track Record
Variable Annuity

Matching

a. rental real estate
b. risk return ratio
c. 3-5 year track record
d. 5-10 year track record
e. annuity
f. risk
g. small-cap
h. large-cap
i. diversification
j. share
k. portfolio

____ 1. Growth and Income Funds

____ 2. Always check this record when investing

____ 3. Spread around the risk

____ 4. Piece of ownership in company stock

____ 5. List of your investments

____ 6. Least liquid of all investments

____ 7. Degree of uncertainty of the return on an investment

____ 8. Aggressive Growth Funds

____ 9. Savings account within an insurance company

____ 10. Risk goes up, return goes up

Multiple Choice

11. Liquidity means to spread around and lower risk.
    a. true
    b. false

12. A single stock is the best place to keep your emergency fund.
    a. true
    b. false

13. A certificate of deposit is the best place to keep an emergency fund.
    a. true
    b. false

14. Diversification lowers your risk with investing.
    a. true
    b. false

15. Commodities and futures are extremely speculative and carry a high risk.
    a. true
    b. false

16. __% of any 10-year period in the stock market has made money.
    a. 53
    b. 97
    c. 75
    d. 100

17. Long-term investments properly diversified include the following mutual funds:
    a. growth, growth and income, bond, aggressive growth
    b. growth, balanced, international, bond
    c. international, bond, aggressive growth, growth
    d. growth, growth and income, international, aggressive growth

18. What is the KISS rule of investing?
    a. Keep It Simple Stocks
    b. Keep It Simple Stupid
    c. Keep It Solo Situated
    d. Keep It Somewhere Safe

19. Which of the following is not a good investment?
    a. gold
    b. viaticals
    c. futures
    d. all of the above

20. Which statement is true about liquidity?
    a. the less liquid the investment, the less return
    b. the more liquid an investment, the more return
    c. the more liquid an investment, the less return
    d. both a and b

21. Which one is not a type of annuity:
    a. variable
    b. stable
    c. fixed
    d. none of the above

22. A savings account with a certificate is a:
    a. bond
    b. annuity
    c. C.D.
    d. viatical

Short Answer

23. Why do you look at the long-term track record with a mutual fund?

24. What are some investments that don't give you a high rate of return?

25. List four types of investments that you should always avoid.

26. How do you go about finding the right person to help you invest?

27. What was the most important fact or idea about investing that you learned in this lesson?

28. Name one thing from this lesson that you could apply to your life right now.

29. Daniel just graduated from college and wants to invest 15% of his income into mutual funds. He earns an annual salary of $32,000 but is $21,000 in debt with his car and student loan. He has $500 in savings. What steps does Daniel need to take?

30. How are single stocks different from mutual funds and which is the better investment?

Case Studies

31. John is 63 years old, owns his house and is a little bit anxious about whether he has enough money for retirement. He is considering borrowing $20,000 against his home to invest in a series of aggressive growth stock mutual funds. The track record for these funds over the last 3 years has been an average growth rate of 21.2%. The interest rate on the loan would only be 7.5%. Should John do this to help with his retirement?

32. Candace and Mike just inherited $25,000 from a relative and are really excited about investing it and watching it grow. However, they still have $10,000 worth of debt to pay from credit cards. Before Dave gives them financial advice, he asks them one question. What question does he ask them? What financial advice does he then give them?

33. Brooke's friend has been bugging her to invest in gold. She says it has been trading really high and will only continue to go up in value. Brooke has $1,000 that she is ready to invest. She knows you listen to Dave's show and wants to know what he would say. What would you tell her?

WEALTH BUILDING and COLLEGE SAVINGS

What do other high school students know about wealth building?

We asked high school students what they would do with an extra $5,000.

> "I'd either **buy a used car** or put it in the bank so it can **grow**.
>
> Junior, Michigan

"I would put half in long term-savings, $2,000 in a college fund, and spend $500."

Senior, Wyoming

"I'd put half in a mutual fund, $1,000 in savings, $1,000 in a money market, and buy a gaming system with the rest."

Senior, Missouri

"I would save it until I was 18, then put a down payment on a house and rent it for profit."

Senior, Texas

"Save $3,500 and shop with the rest."

Junior, Alabama

LEARNING OUTCOMES

Explain what is meant by "tax-favored dollars."

List the different types of retirement plans.

Differentiate between a traditional and Roth IRA.

Illustrate how a 401(k) company match works and prioritize money into various investments.

Describe how pre-tax and after-tax investments work.

KEY TERMS

401(k)
ESA
IRA
Pre-Tax
Rollover
Roth IRA
Tax-Favored Dollars

BEFORE YOU BEGIN

What do you know about Wealth Building and College Savings?

Before you watch the lesson on Wealth Building and College Savings, think about what you already know. The word bank below contains some of the bigger concepts that you will learn in this lesson. Complete the first two columns before watching Dave's lesson as you work through the chapter. Fill in the last column with the details you learned.

	I **think** I know:	I **want** to know:	What I **learned:**
401(k)			
Roth IRA			
ESA			
UTMA/UGMA			
Before Tax			
After Tax			
Rule of 72			
Pension			

Retirement and College Funding

Once the emergency fund is in place, you should begin retirement and college funding, which falls within long-term investing for _____ _____.

Baby Step 1 is _____ in the bank.

Baby Step 2 is _____ _____.

Baby Step 3 is _____ months of expenses in an emergency fund.

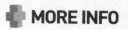 Baby Step 4 is investing 15% of your household income into Roth IRAs and pre-tax retirement plans.

Invest _____% of your household income into Roth IRAs and pre-tax retirement plans.

Tax-favored means that the investment is in a _____ _____ or has a special tax treatment.

MORE INFO

The Federal Deposit Insurance Corporation (FDIC) is responsible for insuring or guaranteeing deposits in banks and savings institutions up to $250,000. It was created in 1933 to restore public confidence after thousands of banks failed.

The Federal Reserve—sometimes called "The Fed"—is the central banking system of the United States and has four main duties:

1. It carries out the nation's monetary policies by managing the supply of money.

2. It supervises and regulates banking institutions.

3. It maintains the stability of the financial system.

4. It provides financial services to banks.

! STUPID TAX

"I paid over $200 for a snowboard because I loved the design. I never even used it once because it turned out to be too small."

Senior, Wyoming

"I bought a guitar when I should have paid for my speeding ticket."

Senior, Florida

"I saved up to buy an expensive hair straightener only to find my old, cheap straightener worked way better."

Junior, Missouri

Qualified Plans

▶ Individual Retirement Arrangement (_____)
▶ Simplified Employee Pension Plan (_____)
▶ 401(k), 403(b), 457

Individual Retirement Arrangements

When it comes to IRAs, everyone with an _____ income is eligible.

The maximum annual contribution for income earners is $_____ as of 2008.

Remember: IRA is not a type of _____ at a bank. It is the tax treatment on virtually any type of investment.

Roth IRA

The Roth IRA is an _____-tax IRA that grows tax _____.

$ MONEY FACTS

The Roth IRA is named for Senator William Roth of Delaware, who authored this section of the Taxpayer Relief Act of 1997.

Why the Roth IRA?

The Roth IRA has more _____.

Higher _____ at retirement.

Investing $5,000 pre-tax is different than investing $5,000 _____ tax. It takes more than $5,000 to get home with $5,000 after tax. It would take $_____.

There are no taxes when you cash it out, so it forces you to _____ more.

It has tons of _____.

Who Is Eligible:

▶ Singles—100% contribution with income less than $95,000. Phase out between $95,000-$110,000. Not eligible above $110,000.

▶ Married filed jointly—100% contribution with income less than $150,000. Phase out between $150,000-$160,000. Not eligible over $160,000.

Flexibility of a Roth IRA:

▶ Tax-free and penalty-free withdrawals at any time equal to contributions. After the emergency fund is depleted, you have a fall back.

▶ After five years, you can make tax-free, penalty-free withdrawals for 100% under these conditions:
1. Over 59 and a half years old

$ MONEY FACTS

The average graduate of a four-year college has student loan debt of **$19,237.** Graduate students pile on even more student loan debt, ranging up to **$114,000.**

Miles To Go

Nearly **half** of all Americans (46%) have less than **$10,000** saved for retirement.

Miles To Go

37% of teens notice their parents being concerned about retirement.

Charles Schwab Survey

Only **13%** of teens know what a 401 (k) plan is.

Charles Schwab Survey

29% of teens feel knowledgeable about knowing how to pay for college.

Charles Schwab Survey

49% of teens say they're concerned their parents/ guardians will not be able to support them financially if they attend college.

Charles Schwab Survey

2. Because of death or disability

3. First-time home purchase
   (max $10,000)

END OF VIDEO PART 1

Simplified Employee Pension Plan (SEPP)

A _____-employed person may deduct up to _____% of their net profit on the business by investing in a SEPP.

▸ The maximum deductible amount is $45,000 (as of 2007) and all employees who have been with the firm more than three of the last five years must receive the same percentage of their pay into a retirement plan.

 REAL LIFE

Winning the lottery does not guarantee peace of mind when it comes to your financial future. In fact, Ellen Goodstein of bankrate.com reported that just the opposite happened to some lottery winners—they went broke.

Saving and investing have nothing to do with the amount of money you make or get. It is about making it a priority and being smart with your money.

William Post won $16.2 million from the Pennsylvania Lottery in 1988
- His former girlfriend sued him and won a share of his winnings.
- His brother was arrested for hiring a hit man to kill him, hoping to inherit the winnings.
- His other siblings harassed him until he invested in a car business and restaurant, both of which failed.
- He was $1 million in debt just one year later.
- Ultimately, he declared bankruptcy and now lives on food stamps.

Willie Hurt won $3.1 million from the Michigan Lottery in 1989
- He spent his money on a divorce and crack cocaine.
- Two years later, he was broke and facing murder charges.

Suzanne Mullins won $4.2 million from the Virginia Lottery in 1993
- She borrowed $197,746, using her lottery winnings as collateral.
- She stopped making payments on the loan after she collected the rest of her winnings in a lump sum.
- The company Suzanne borrowed the money from won a judgment against her for $154,147, but has never seen a dime.
- Today, she has no assets.

401(k), 403(b) & 457 Retirement Plans

Most companies have completely done away with traditional _____ plans.

It has been replaced by self-_____ and _____ plans, like the 401(k).

▶ The 401(k) is yours, unlike the pension plan which was an asset of the company. If the company went broke, you most likely lost your pension.

▶ If you don't put money into a 401(k) there will be nothing in the fund. A pension, however, is funded automatically by your company.

The 403(b) is found in non-profit organizations such as churches, hospitals and schools.

The 457 is _____ compensation, which means you are deferring or putting off compensation. Usually this is available for government employees.

Do not use a _____ Investment Contract (GIC) or bond funds to fund your plan.

▶ This is like a C.D. inside of your 401(k). You will only make about 3-4% and it will not help you win long-term.

You should be funding your plan whether your company _____ or not.

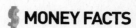

MONEY FACTS

The **Rule of 72** is a quick way to do compound interest problems in your head. It isn't exact, but it will give you a quick benchmark to see how long it will take to double your money at a given interest rate.

The **Rule of 72** says that by dividing the interest rate into 72, it will tell you approximately how many years it will take to double your money.

Example: How long will it take to double your money at 12%?

72/12 = 6 years

What interest rate do I need to earn if I want my money to double in 7 years?

72/7=10.28%

Imagine if a 30 year old couple puts $500 a month into a ROTH IRA at 12% interest. When they reach age 70, they will have $5,154,854 in TAX FREE money!

Imagine if that same couple instead puts $500 a month into a ROTH 401(k) at 12%. When they reach age 70, they will have $5,154,854 in TAX FREE money!

Now, imagine if the same couple funds both their ROTH IRA and ROTH 401(k) at the same time. After 40 years of saving $1,000 a month, they will have $10,309,708 in TAX FREE money at the age of 70!

Rollovers

You should always _____ over retirement plans to an _____ when you leave the company.

Don't bring the money home, instead, move it straight into an IRA by a _____ _____.

Roll to a Roth Only If:

1. You will have over $700,000 by age 65.

2. You can afford to pay the _____ separately, not from the IRA.

3. You understand all _____ will become due on the rollover amount.

> END OF VIDEO PART 2

Retirement Loans

Never _____ on your retirement plan. NEVER!

Federal Thrift Plan

For federal government workers who have the standard thrift plan, we recommend 60% in the C fund, 20% in the S fund, and 20% in the I fund.

Baby Step 4

Invest 15% of household income into Roth IRAs and pre-tax retirement.

1. Fund 401(k) or other employer plan up to the _____. (If applicable)

2. Above the match, fund _____ IRAs. If there is no match, start with Roth IRAs.

3. Complete 15% of income by going back to your _____ or other company plans. **◀ END OF VIDEO PART 3**

There are no fill-in-the-blanks for Part 4. **◀ END OF VIDEO PART 4**

College Funding

 Save for your children's education using tax-favored plans.

First...

Save for college by first using Educational Savings Accounts (ESA), nicknamed "Education _____."

You may save $2,000 (after tax) per year, per child, that grows tax free! So, if you start when your child is born and save $2,000 a year for 18 years, you would only invest a total of $36,000. However, at 12% growth, your child would have $126,000 for college—TAX FREE!

REAL LIFE

Scholarships aren't just for the highest scorers on the ACT or SAT. Schools and foundations have broadened their criteria to include community involvement, after-school work and financial status in addition to the traditional athletics and diversity scholarships. Don't avoid the scholarship applications requiring essays. It is a good way to improve your writing skills while earning scholarships. Here are some additional resources to look into.

1. Talk to your guidance counselor.

2. Explore your state's website.

3. Many businesses have scholarships for employee's children. Ask your parents to check at their place of employment.

4. Explore the federal government's website at studentaid.ed.gov

5. Check out the big college organizations for information (collegeboard.com, petersons.com).

6. Apply for scholarships with local organizations such as Rotary Clubs.

"I am 22 and I've been thinking about going back to school. My employer is willing to pay for nine credit hours per semester, but if I take more than nine hours they won't pay anything. My parents think we should get student loans. What do you think?"

DAVE'S ANSWER: I'm sure your parents are good people. And I know they don't mean any real harm. They're just being normal, but in today's culture normal is broke. They've probably been around student loans, car payments and credit cards all their lives, and that's sad.

Go for it! You have a great opportunity staring at you. I mean, how many times does someone offer to pay for your degree with no financial strings attached? You couldn't take much more than nine hours per semester and still work a full-time job anyway.

Above that...

If you want to save more or if you don't meet the income limits for an ESA, use a certain type of _____ plan.

Never buy a plan that:

    1. _____ your options.

    2. Automatically changes your investments based on the _____ of the child.

Only then...

Move to an _____ or _____ plan.

▶ While this is one way to save with reduced taxes, it is _____ as good as the other options.

▶ UTMA/UGMA stands for Uniform _____ / Gift to _____ Act.

▶ The account is _____ in the child's name and a _____ is named, usually the parent or grandparent. This person is the manager until the child reaches age 21. At age 21 (age 18 for UGMA), they can do with it what they please.

Three "Nevers" of College Savings

Never save for college using _____.

Never save for college using _____ bonds. (Only earns 5-6%)

Never save for college using _____ tuition.

An ESA is *not* the right savings vehicle if you need the money within five years. Use a money market mutual fund.

END OF VIDEO PART 5

Recap and Review

Save long-term in tax favored plans—a Roth IRA grows tax-free.

Contribute to your 401(k), especially when a match is offered.

Do not sign up for investment plans that you don't understand.

NEVER borrow on your retirement plan.

You do not have to get a student loan to go to college!

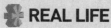
REAL LIFE

You don't *have* to get a student loan to go to college. There are many other ways to pay for higher education besides going into debt. Consider these options instead:

▶ Work while going through school

▶ Get a job on campus

▶ Join the military

▶ Find a job where they will pay for your schooling (ie: UPS)

▶ Go to school in-state as opposed to out-of-state

▶ Go to a public school instead of a private school

▶ Get your core classes at a local community college, then go to a 4-year institution

▶ Live at home while going to college

▶ Get a degree in a field that will help pay for your college (ie: teachers might qualify for tuition grants as long as they agree to teach for 3 or more years)

Vocabulary

401(k)
403(b)
457 Plan
529 Plan
Custodian
Direct Transfer
ESA
IRA
Pre-Paid Tuition
Rollover
Roth IRA
SEPP
Tax-Favored Dollars
UGMA
UTMA

Matching

a. ESA
b. 403(b)
c. 401(k)
d. Roth IRA
e. SEPP

____ 1. Retirement plan for self-employed people

____ 2. Grows tax-free

____ 3. The typical retirement plan found in most corporations

____ 4. Used for college savings

____ 5. The typical retirement plan found in non-profit groups such as schools and hospitals

True/False

____ 6. Pre-tax means the government is letting you invest money before taxes have been taken out.

____ 7. Savings bonds are a good way to save for college.

____ 8. Never borrow money from your retirement plan.

____ 9. When you leave a company, don't move your money from the retirement account.

____ 10. An IRA is a specific type of investment.

Multiple Choice

11. The_____IRA grows tax-free.
    a. Roth
    b. traditional
    c. original
    d. life insurance

12. An Educational Savings Account (ESA) is used for _____ .
    a. retirement
    b. college
    c. an emergency fund
    d. a new car

13. Which of the following is not a retirement plan?
    a. 529
    b. 401(k)
    c. 403(b)
    d. 457

14. Which is not a benefit of the Roth IRA?
    a. grows tax-free
    b. unlimited contributions
    c. provides penalty-free withdrawals under certain circumstances
    d. more choices

15. If your company provides a 100% match up to 6%, how much should you personally contribute to your 401(k) if you earn $35,000 (not including the money the company contributed)?
    a. $1,750
    b. $2,100
    c. $3,500
    d. $5,250

16. If you contribute $2,300 to your 401(k) and your company matches up to 3%, how much is in the account (assume you have not gone over the 3% match)?
    a. $1,150
    b. $2,300
    c. $4,600
    d. $6,900

17. What should you do with your retirement accounts when you leave a company?
    a. cash them out
    b. fund deposit
    c. fund shift
    d. direct transfer

18. Never save for college using:
    a. pre-tax dollars
    b. pre-paid tuition
    c. savings bonds
    d. both b and c

19. Baby Step 5 is:
    a. 3-6 months of expenses saved
    b. college funding
    c. 15% of household income into retirement plans
    d. the debt snowball

20. If Carol and Joe are debt free, how much should they be investing in retirement plans if their combined income is $145,000?
    a. $14,500
    b. $21,000
    c. $21,750
    d. $43,500

Short Answer

21. What are the advantages of a Roth IRA?

22. What is Baby Step 4 and why does your emergency fund have to be fully funded before you begin this step?

23. List some ways you can avoid student loan debt if you do not have a college fund.

24. Why should you take a 401(k) match (if a company offers one) before you start a Roth IRA?

25. Explain what is meant by tax-favored dollars.

26. Why worry about retirement when every worker pays into Social Security?

27. Explain how the rule of 72 works.

Case Studies

28. Courtney and Joe have been saving for their two son's college (age 17 & 15) and now have $16,000 in each account. However, the money is in a savings account. They recently started listening to Dave and realized that is not where their money should be. Does Dave advise them to move the money and if so, where?

29. Jane makes $85,000 at her current job. Her company matches 100% up to 3% and 50% up to 6%. Jane is currently funding her 401(k) at only 10% although she is completely debt free. What does Dave tell her to do for retirement? (Break it down in terms of how much she should be investing total, what the company is matching, and where to put her investments.)

30. Austin and Kayla have $35,000 in debt (student loan, credit cards, car loan) but have cut up all of their credit cards and started their debt snowball. Austin just got a substantial raise and their household income is now $125,000 ($3,500 more per month, net). Should he cash out his 401(k) which has about $25,000, pay off his debt, and start again from square one? Explain your answer.

UNIT 2
CREDIT and DEBT

DANGERS of DEBT

What do other high school students know about debt?

We asked high school students if they or someone they knew ever bought something they couldn't afford.

> "My mom bought a new car and couldn't afford the payments. **The bank repossessed the car.**
>
> Junior, Michigan"

"My friend bought a new car and had to sell it one month later. "

Junior, Tennessee

"I used all my money on an iPod and had none left for gas. I had to borrow money from my parents so I could make it to work."

Senior, Missouri

"My cousin bought a really expensive car and she can't make the payments"

Junior, Alabama

"A friend bought a car he couldn't afford. After making only a few payments, the car got repossessed."

Junior, Missouri

LEARNING OUTCOMES

Analyze the history and evolution of credit.

Demonstrate the various ways people get into debt.

Compare and contrast credit cards and debit cards.

Explain how the debt snowball works.

Evaluate and refute the myths associated with debt.

KEY TERMS

Annual Fee
Annual Percentage Rate
Credit
Debt Snowball
Depreciation
Tax Deduction

What do you know about the dangers of debt?

Before watching the lesson, read each statement below and mark whether you agree or disagree in the "before" column. Then, after watching the lesson, do it again using the "after" column to see if you changed your mind on any question.

Before			After		
Agree	Disagree			Agree	Disagree
☐	☐	1. Co-signing a loan is a good way to help a friend or relative.		☐	☐
☐	☐	2. Cash advance and title pawning are needed services but should be used with caution.		☐	☐
☐	☐	3. The typical millionaire drives reliable, used cars.		☐	☐
☐	☐	4. Leasing a car is a smart way to drive a newer car for a lower monthly payment.		☐	☐
☐	☐	5. A new car is the largest purchase most consumers make that goes down in value.		☐	☐
☐	☐	6. A home equity loan is a substitute for an emergency fund and a good way to consolidate debt.		☐	☐
☐	☐	7. You need to have a credit card to rent a car or check in to a hotel.		☐	☐
☐	☐	8. It is OK to use a credit card if you pay it off every month.		☐	☐
☐	☐	9. Teens are the number one target of credit card companies today.		☐	☐
☐	☐	10. You spend more money when you pay with cash than when you use credit cards.		☐	☐

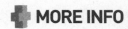

4 DANGERS of DEBT

Debt Is Everywhere

According to *The Wall Street Journal*, _____% of Americans are living paycheck to paycheck.

When it comes to debt, if you tell a lie or spread a _____ long enough, eventually it becomes accepted as the _____.

Debt has been _____ to us with such intensity for so long that to imagine living without it requires a complete _____ shift, a completely new way of looking at things.

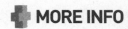
MORE INFO

When someone borrows money from another, we understand they have an obligation to repay. A study in the dictionary will show you what this really means. A definition of obligation is "bound," which is defined as "tied; in bonds: a bound prisoner."

"The rich rule over the poor, and the borrower is slave to the lender." (Proverbs 22:7) Don't become a prisoner or slave to debt!

History of Credit

▶ 1910: In the Sears catalog, credit was called "folly."

J.C. Penney didn't believe in debt and would not allow credit to be given in his stores. It wasn't until after his death in 1971 that credit was widely accepted in the J.C. Penney stores.

Henry Ford of Ford Motor Company hated debt and would not offer credit on cars for 10 years after General Motors began offering credit.

WISE GUYS

"Most people have the will to win, few have the will to prepare to win."

Bobby Knight

▶ 1950: This was the birth of what is now known as the credit card; Frank McNamara established partnerships with several New York City restaurants. His goal was to allow patrons the ability to pay for meals with a single payment card—the first credit card. McNamara's company, Diners Club, is still in business today.

▶ 1958: A West Coast bank, the Bank of America, issued a little piece of plastic called the BankAmericard to its customers. Later that year, American Express was born.

▶ 1970: Only 15% of Americans owned credit cards.

▶ 1976: BankAmericard changed its name to Visa.

▶ 1986: Sears got into a dispute with Visa over the fee structure. As a result, Sears created their own brand, the Discover Card. This quickly became the most profitable division of Sears.

Debt Through the Generations

Our **great grandparents** thought debt was a sin.

Our **grandparents** thought it was stupid.

Our **parents** borrowed on a few things.

We borrow on everything!

END OF VIDEO PART 1

Debunking the Myths

Myth 1

▶ MYTH: If I _____ money to a friend or relative, I will be helping them.

▶ TRUTH: The relationship will be strained or _____. `END OF VIDEO PART 2`

Myth 2

▶ MYTH: By _____ a loan, I am helping out a friend or relative.

▶ TRUTH: The bank requires a cosigner because the person isn't likely to _____. Be ready to pay the loan and have your credit damaged.

Myth 3

▶ MYTH: _____ _____, rent-to-own, title pawning, and tote-the-note lots are needed _____ for lower income people to help them get ahead.

▶ TRUTH: These are horrible, greedy rip-offs that aren't needed and benefit no one but the owners of these companies.

80% of _____ in America are first-generation rich. That means they started out with nothing, did smart stuff, and became millionaires. That's the opposite of what we're talking about here.

"I'm going to college after I graduate and will need a credit card for various things, such as internet access. Can you recommend one that's better than the others?"

DAVE'S ANSWER:

I never recommend using credit cards. NEVER! You can obtain Internet access, make online purchases, and buy things in a store with a debit card.

Using a debit card, which is connected to your checking account, means you're spending money that's actually yours. You're not borrowing it from some bank and then paying interest on it. If you don't have money in your account, you won't be making purchases. That's the way it works and it's the smartest thing you can do.

Credit cards are the quickest way I know to become broke and stay broke for the rest of your life!

MONEY FACTS

New car dealers make the following profit:

$82 for the cash sale of a new car

$775 for financing a new car

$1,300 for leasing a new car

Smart Money Magazine

Myth 4

▶ MYTH: The _____ and other forms of gambling will make me _____.

▶ TRUTH: The lottery is a _____ on the poor and on people who can't do math.

Texas Tech University did a study on the Texas Lottery and found that people without a high school diploma spent an average of _____a month playing the lottery. College graduates spent _____ a month on average.

When studies are done on the lottery, it's always the lower-income ZIP codes that generate the highest revenue or sales. **END OF VIDEO PART 3**

Myth 5

▶ MYTH: _____ payments are a way of life and you'll always have one.

▶ TRUTH: Staying away from car payments by driving reliable used cars is what the typical _____ does. That is how they became millionaires.

The average car payment today is $464 per month over 64 months.

Myth 6

▶ MYTH: _____ your car is what sophisticated financial people do. You should always lease things that go down in value. There are tax advantages.

▶ TRUTH: *Consumer Reports*, *Smart Money* magazine and a good calculator will tell you that the car _____ is the most _____ way to finance and operate a vehicle.

 **MORE INFO**

Secured loans and unsecured loans are the two types of loans typically available to borrowers.

An **unsecured loan** is given to borrowers based on their financial resources or ability to repay the loan. Nothing "secures" the loan. In other words, the lender does not have rights to a specific asset if the loan is not repaid. Personal loans, student loans, and personal lines of credit are examples of unsecured loans.

A **secured loan** is usually needed when borrowing large amounts of money. The loan is "secured" with collateral. In other words, if you default on the loan and your house was used as collateral, the lender would take the house. Secured loans usually have lower interest rates and longer repayment terms. Automobile loans, mortgages, and home equity loans are examples of secured loans.

"My credit card has no annual fee and I get money back from the credit card company for all of my charges. I only use it for bills and I pay it off every month. So, I'm getting money from the credit card company for using their credit card. What's wrong with that?"

DAVE'S ANSWER:

I've been doing financial counseling for decades and I've worked with tens of thousands of people. During that time, I've repeatedly met folks who were doing exactly what you are doing and it has come back to bite them.

When you're talking about credit cards, you're talking about a multi-billion dollar industry designed to do just one thing—separate you from your money. And they're really good at it! They're more than willing to pay you a percentage point back because they know you're going to stumble at some point—and that's when they pounce!

I've talked with hundreds of millionaires, and I've never met one who said they got rich thanks to credit card rebates. They've all just gone about the business of earning money, living on less than they make, and saving. They don't play with snakes because they know, sooner or later, they'll get bitten.

WISE GUYS

"If you want to be well off financially, quit buying stuff!"

Anonymous

If you own a business, you can _____ _____ your paid-for car on taxes without paying payments for the privilege.

The way to _____ the money lost on things that go down in value is to buy slightly _____ .

▶ END OF VIDEO PART 4

Myth 7

▶ MYTH: You can get a good deal on a _____ car.

▶ TRUTH: A new car loses _____ of its value in the first four years. This is the largest purchase most consumers make that goes down in value.

On average, a $28,000 car will be worth $8,400 in four years.

Myth 8

▶ MYTH: I'll take out a 30-year mortgage and pay _____.

▶ TRUTH: Life happens and something else will always seem more important. Never take out more than a _____ year fixed-rate mortgage.

30-Year vs. 15-Year Mortgage at 6%

$250,000 Home - $25,000 Down Payment = $225,000 Mortgage Amount

	PAYMENT	TOTAL	PAY BACK
30 years		$1,349	$485,636
15 years		$1,899	$341,762
Difference		$ 550	$143,874

A 15-Year Mortgage Saved More Than $143,000!

 **FEEDBACK**

Have you ever loaned someone money, only to have it turn into a bad experience?

"My friendship hasn't been the same since I loaned a friend money and didn't get it back. I don't trust him anymore."

Junior, Missouri

"A close friend of mine bought a new car and couldn't afford the payment. I loaned him $300, then he left the state. I couldn't afford to take him to court because of court costs, so I dropped the whole thing."

Junior, Michigan

"I loaned $150 to a friend who never returned it and then claimed that I 'gave' it to him."

Senior, Missouri

"I loaned my mother over $2,000 to help pay for my 19-year-old brother's car note and college fees. She promised to pay me back but it has been over a year and a half and I haven't received one payment from her. I will never loan money again."

Senior, Georgia

REAL LIFE

Sadly, it is easier than ever for 18-year-old college students to get credit cards. According to the Jump$tart Coalition for Personal Financial Literacy, students entering college are offered an average of eight credit card solicitations in their first week of school. In 2006, students received an average of 25-50 credit card offers per semester, according to the United College Marketing Services.

In 2001, CBS's *60 Minutes* correspondent Vicky Mabrey reported on the devastating effects credit card marketing had for one college student and his mother.

Sean Moyer was an 18-year-old National Merit Scholar with future law school plans when he headed off to the University of Texas in Dallas. Even though he had always worked from the time he was 16, Sean was naïve when it came to credit cards.

Like a lot of other freshmen, Sean applied for and received his first credit card when he got to college. Because of credit card debt, Sean was forced to transfer to the University of Oklahoma so he could live at home. By this time, he was working two jobs making minimum wage as a salesperson and gift wrapper for a major department store.

One day, his mother knocked on Sean's door but got no answer. Upon entering, she found him dead; he had hung himself in the closet. Sean Moyer was 22 at the time with $14,000 of credit card debt. His mother told *60 Minutes*, "It just never occurred to me that you could give a credit card to an 18-year-old making minimum wage. When he died, he had 12 credit cards." In 2007, CNN ran a similar story about credit card marketing on campuses and what happened to Sean Moyer. They reported that Sean's mother still receives credit card offers in the mail for her son, despite the fact that he died in 1998.

Myth 9

▶ MYTH: It's wise to take out an _____ or a _____ mortgage if "I know I'll be moving."

▶ TRUTH: You *will* be moving when they _____.

▶ The adjustable-rate mortgage is here to keep the _____ from losing money. It transfers the _____ of higher interest rates to you.

END OF VIDEO PART 5

Myth 10

▸ MYTH: You need a _____ _____ to rent a car or make _____ online or by phone.

▸ TRUTH: A _____ card does all of that.

Myth 11

▸ MYTH: I pay my _____ _____ off every month with no annual payment or fee. I get brownie points, air miles and a free hat.

▸ TRUTH: When you use cash instead of plastic, you spend _____ less because spending cash hurts.

According to carddata.com, U.S. consumers racked up an estimated $51 billion worth of fast food on their personal credit and debit cards in 2006, compared to $33.2 billion one year ago.

Myth 12

▸ MYTH: I'll make sure my _____ gets a credit card so he or she can learn to be responsible with money.

▸ TRUTH: Teens are a huge _____ of credit card companies today. ▸ END OF VIDEO PART 6

$ MONEY FACTS

Before McDonald's chose to accept credit cards, the average ticket price was $4.75. When they went to credit cards, the average ticket price went to $7.00. That's a **47%** increase!

Nightline, ABC

Researchers studying the neurological impact of big purchases hooked up an MRI to participants and watched their brainwave activity. They found that when people **spend cash** it neurologically registers as **pain.**

Carnegie Mellon Magazine

Credit cards are moving away from a magnetic swipe and moving towards chips in the cards. It's called **RFID** technology and all you have to do when you use your credit card is wave it.

💲 MONEY FACTS

88% of teens don't like the way it feels to owe someone money.

29% of teens are already in debt with the average amount owed at **$293.**

Only **41%** are concerned about paying back the money they owe.

29% of teens would prefer buying things with a credit card versus cash.

51% of teens agree that it is easier to buy things with a credit card than cash.

25% of teens say their parents/guardians are more likely to use a credit card than cash.

36% of teens believe that their parents/guardians are concerned about paying credit card bills.

Charles Schwab Survey

As soon as you get to college, you will receive offers from credit card companies. About 80% of college graduates have credit card debt before they even get a job.

Myth 13

▶ MYTH: The home equity loan is good for _____ and is a substitute for the emergency fund.

▶ TRUTH: You don't go into _____ for emergencies.

Myth 14

▶ MYTH: Debt _____ saves interest and you get a smaller _____.

▶ TRUTH: Debt consolidation is a _____.

Debt consolidation saves little or no _____ because you will throw your low interest loans into the deal.

You cannot _____ your way out of debt!

_____ payments equal more _____ in debt.

Myth 15

▶ MYTH: Debt is a _____. It should be used to create prosperity.

▶ TRUTH: The _____ is slave to the lender.

When surveyed, the Forbes 400 were asked, "What is the most important key to building wealth?" _____ replied that becoming and staying _____ free was the number one key to wealth building.

 END OF VIDEO PART 7

Steps Out of Debt

1. Quit _____ more _____!

2. You must _____ money.

3. _____ something.

4. Part-time _____ or _____ (temporarily)

5. Use the _____ _____.

Baby Step 2

 Pay off all debt using the debt snowball.

💬 **FEEDBACK**

"I'm 23 years old and just getting started. I finished Baby Step 1 last week and am now onto tackling $2,700 in credit card debt. After that, it will be $17,000 in student loans. I, too, am grateful to be on this path now—and not 30 years from now."

Missouri

"I'm 23, $17,000 in debt, and miserable."

Michigan

"I make about $30,000 a year and owe $20,000 on my car. I was at $27,000 a year ago, so I'm getting there slowly but surely! I made a big mistake buying a new car and now I'm paying for it."

Texas

"I'm 22 and on Baby Step 2. I have about $2,200 left on a credit card and then $15,000 for my car and $20,000 in student loans. I currently work full-time plus overtime while running a small eBay business on the side."

Georgia

Debt Snowball

Now it's time to knock out that debt! List your debts in order, from the smallest balance to the largest. Don't be concerned with interest rates, unless two debts have a similar payoff balance. In that case, list the one with the higher interest rate first. As you start eliminating debts, you'll start to build some serious momentum. These quick wins will keep you motivated, so you'll be able to stay on track.

The idea of the snowball is simple: pay minimum payments on all of your debts except for the smallest one. Then, attack that one with gazelle intensity! Every extra dollar you can get your hands on should be thrown at that smallest debt until it is gone. Then, you attack the second one. Every time you pay a debt off, you add its old minimum payment to your next debt payment. So, as the snowball rolls over, it picks up more snow. Get it?

Redo this sheet every time you pay off a debt so that you can see how close you're getting to total debt freedom. The "New Payment" is the total of the previous debt's payment PLUS the current debt's minimum. As these payments compound, you'll start making huge payments as you work down the list.

ITEM	TOTAL PAYOFF	MINIMUM PAYMENT	NEW PAYMENT
JC Penney	$150	$15	(Garage Sale)
Sears	$250	$10	$25
Visa	$500	$75	$100
MasterCard	$1,500	$90	$190
Car	$4,000	$210	$400
Student Loan	$4,000	$65	$465

Recap and Review

Debt is heavily marketed to young people. You will receive a lot of offers from credit card companies.

The fastest-growing group of bankruptcy filers consist of people under 25 years old.

Car payments do not have to be a way of life.

You do not need to build your credit score by applying for a credit card.

The best way to beat debt is to quit borrowing money and live on less than you make.

Vocabulary

Annual Fee
Annual Percentage Rate
ARM
Balloon Mortgage
Credit
Credit Card
Credit Limit
Debit Card
Debt Consolidation
Debt Snowball
Depreciation
Finance Charge
Foreclose
Grace Period
Home Equity Loan
Introductory Rate
Lease
Loan Term
Myth
Paradigm
Tax Deduction

Matching

a. debt consolidation
b. co-signing
c. debt snowball
d. leasing
e. cash advance
f. paradigm
g. adjustable rate mortgage
h. home equity loan
i. credit

____ 1. A different way of looking at something

____ 2. Charges of 400% and up for their services

____ 3. Money loaned

____ 4. Using your home as collateral to borrow money

____ 5. Taking responsibility for someone else's loan.

____ 6. Combining debt into one payment

____ 7. Long-term rental agreement

True or False

_____ 8. Debt consolidation is wise.

_____ 9. You need a credit card to rent a car.

_____ 10. Buying used cars is a good way to minimize depreciation.

_____ 11. The typical millionaire drives new cars.

_____ 12. The elderly are the number one target of credit card companies.

_____ 13. Co-signing a loan is a way to help out a friend or relative.

_____ 14. The lottery is a tax on the poor and on people who can't do math.

_____ 15. Home equity loans are a good way to consolidate debt.

_____ 16. It is never wise to take out an ARM or balloon mortgage.

_____ 17. Paying off the balance of your credit card each month is an acceptable use of credit.

_____ 18. The best way to teach teenagers about money is to get them a credit card.

_____ 19. It is best to attack your debt by consolidating many payments into one.

_____ 20. Carrying cash results in an increase of spending versus paying with credit.

Short Answer

21. Why do people go into debt when they know that they will have to pay more for an item once they figure interest?

22. Why are teens such a major target of the credit card industry?

23. How do cash advance and car title companies keep people in the cycle of debt?

24. Why is it better to buy a used car instead of a brand new vehicle?

25. Why does debt consolidation typically not save money?

26. Explain how the debt snowball works.

27. What are the five steps to get out of debt?

28. How can lending money cause problems in a relationship?

Case Studies

29. Tiffany will graduate from college in December with a degree in elementary education. She already has a teaching job lined up, and it will be the first time in her life that she will make more than minimum wage. She has $15,000 in student loan debt, $6,000 to pay on a car repossession, and $3,000 in credit card debt. How should she handle the salary increase?

30. Thomas owes $438 on his credit card and was unable to pay more than the minimum payment of $20. Unfortunately, he mailed the payment late resulting in a late fee of $39. The interest rate on this card is 26%, compounded monthly. What will his new balance be?

31. Ryan is barely able to keep up with his minimum payments. He has four credit cards, a car payment and a mortgage. He is wondering if he should consolidate all of his debt by taking a low-interest home equity loan. What would Dave tell Ryan to do? How would the interest rate of each debt factor into Dave's advice?

CONSUMER AWARENESS  CH 5

What do other high school students know about consumer awareness?

Companies use clever marketing schemes, like funny television commercials, to entice consumers to buy their products. We asked high school students to share their favorite television commercials:

> " I like the Super Bowl commercials. **It shows how much competition there is between companies.** "
>
> Senior, Utah

"I love the glass cleaner commercial where the birds close the glass door and the man runs into it because he can't see it."

Senior, Alabama

"I like the soft drink ad where the defensive lineman scores and starts dancing."

Senior, Missouri

"My favorite is the airline commercial where the guy throws a rock at a car that's not his."

Senior, Texas

"I like the insurance commercials with the cavemen."

Junior, Missouri

LEARNING OUTCOMES

List the four major ways companies compete for your money.

Evaluate the role opportunity cost plays in purchasing decisions.

Distinguish what constitutes a significant purchase.

List the five steps to take before making a significant purchase.

KEY TERMS

Buyer's Remorse
Financing
Finite
Opportunity Cost
Significant Purchase

BEFORE YOU BEGIN

What do you know about consumer awareness?

How aware are you of the marketing that goes on all around you every day? Answer the following questions before you watch the lesson.

1. What percent of "90 days same-as-cash" purchases are not paid in 90 days and convert to payments?
   ☐ 25%　　☐ 50%　　☐ 75%　　☐ over 75%

2. The average cost of a 30-second television advertisement during the 2007 Super Bowl was:
   ☐ $1 million　　☐ $1.5 million　　☐ $2 million　　☐ over $2 million

3. The average American was exposed to almost 560 advertisements daily in 1971. Today that number is closer to:
   ☐ 1,500　　☐ 2,500　　☐ 3,000　　☐ more than 5,000

4. A Harvard University study found that for every hour of television you watch each week, your yearly spending increases by an average of:
   ☐ $50　　☐ $100　　☐ $200　　☐ $500

5. How much is spent on online advertising directed at kids?
   ☐ $5 billion　　☐ $10 billion　　☐ $15 billion　　☐ $20 billion

How many of these best-known advertising slogans do you know?
Do you know the companies that coined them?

1954　"Melts in your mouth, _____ ___ _____ _____"　　Company:_____

1968　"Things go better with _____"　　Company:_____

1971　"You deserve a _____ _____"　　Company:_____

1973　"Have it your _____"　　Company:_____

1985　"Where's the _____?"　　Company:_____

Buyer Beware

"Caveat Emptor" means _____ _____.

Companies use every angle to aggressively compete for your _____.

Four Major Ways

1. _____ selling.

   END OF VIDEO PART 1

2. _____ as a marketing tool.

   ▶ _____ of "90 days same-as-cash" contracts convert to payments which are usually at 24% APR with rule of 78's prepayment penalty.

3. _____, _____, _____, and other media.

4. Product _____.

   ▶ Brand Recognition

   END OF VIDEO PART 2

   ▶ Color

   ▶ Shelf Position

   ▶ Packaging

$ MONEY FACTS

Over **25%** of Christmas shoppers will still be paying off the bills come next Christmas! The average consumer takes at least six months to pay off holiday bills.

The Wall Street Journal

If a $1,200 tab is charged on a card this season at 17% interest and only the minimum payments are made, it will take almost **20 years** to pay it off and will cost $2,076 extra in interest.

The Wall Street Journal

Credit card issuers spend more than **$150 million** on holiday advertising and promotions.

The Wall Street Journal

For every hour of television per week you watch, you spend an average of **$200.00** extra a year.

Harvard University

"What's the biggest mistake you made when you went broke?"

DAVE'S ANSWER: The biggest mistake I made was going deeply into debt. I didn't understand that debt is not a wealth-building tool, as some people have suggested, but instead was an anchor around my neck.

Debt steals your ability to do something more rewarding—and fun—with your money. For instance, if you borrow $200 to buy a bike and you agree to pay 10% interest, that is $20 in interest that you have to give to someone else. That's $20 you don't have left to spend on a video game, accessories for your bike or even a movie with your friends. You can keep that money for your own use if you're just willing to delay getting that bike long enough to save and pay with cash.

"What's wrong with buying things on 12 months same-as-cash?"

DAVE'S ANSWER: It's a stupid idea. First off, if I buy the item with cash, I'll get a better deal. Plus, if you play with snakes, you'll get bitten. If they record your payment wrong and it's late, they'll backcharge you through the entire term of the deal at about 24-38% interest.

You'll spend the next year and a half cleaning up this mess. It actually happened with one of our clients here. If you can't save up and pay for the item with cash, you can't afford to buy it!

➕ MORE INFO

Have you ever wanted to know what was really important to someone? Look at their checkbook entries. Are they spending a lot on "stuff" like entertainment, clothes, friends, etc? People spend their money on things most meaningful to their heart. "For where your treasure is"—the money you spend or save—"there your heart will be also." (Matthew 6:21)

Significant Purchases

A "significant purchase" is normally anything over _____.

Our bodies go through physiological changes when making a _____ _____.

We all have that spoiled, red-faced, grocery store kid living inside of us. His name is _____.

> END OF VIDEO PART 3

What to Do

You can always spend more than you _____. You must develop _____ over _____ by following these steps:

1. Wait _____ before making a purchase.

2. Consider your buying _____.
   No amount of stuff equals _____ or fulfillment.

   END OF VIDEO PART 4

3. Never buy anything you do not _____.

4. Consider the "_____ _____" of your money.

5. Seek wise _____.

   END OF VIDEO PART 5

Recap and Review

Be aware—companies aggressively market to you and they are experts at getting your money.

Consider your buying motives. No amount of stuff will equal contentment.

Learn the five steps to developing power over purchase.

Always remember, if you can't pay cash, you can't afford it!

Chapter 5: Consumer Awareness **69**

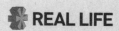

REAL LIFE

Television ads are thought to be the most effective medium for mass market advertising. According to Wikipedia, the first television advertisement in America was broadcast in New York City on July 1, 1941. The Bulova Watch Company paid $9 for a 20-second spot that aired on NBC before a Brooklyn Dodgers and Philadelphia Phillies baseball game.

Fast forward to 2007, where the average half-hour of television contains 22 minutes of programming and eight minutes of commercials. These ads are either national or local, with national being the most expensive spots.

The Super Bowl is known almost more for its commercials than for the football game. The average cost of a 30-second television spot during the 2007 Super Bowl was $2.6 million. The ads reached an estimated 90 million viewers—quite a market and obviously worth the advertising dollars.

Vocabulary

APR
Buyer's Remorse
Brand Recognition
Caveat Emptor
Financing
Finite
Impulse Purchase
Opportunity Cost
Rule of 78
Significant Purchase

Matching

a. buyer beware
b. financing
c. counsel
d. branding
e. overnight
f. opportunity cost
g. 3,000
h. significant purchase

___ 1. Seek wise _____

___ 2. Wait _____ before making a major purchase

___ 3. Borrowing money and paying over time

___ 4. Number of advertisements a person views daily

___ 5. Spend $60 on the latest video game, or give $60 to charity

___ 6. Caveat Emptor

___ 7. An amount of money spent that causes some pain

___ 8. Creates consumer awareness for a trademark or product

True or False

_____ 9. Color is not a product positioning technique used to get the buyer's attention.

_____ 10. Advertising slogans that have been around for a long time no longer work.

11. Answering a question with a question is the sign of a well-trained salesperson.

12. Typically, "90 days same-as-cash" contracts convert to payments with interest up to 24% APR.

13. The opportunity cost of purchasing a new cell phone could be the purchase of a new prom dress.

Want or Need

Using the Four Walls as a guide, indicate which is a want and which is a need.

14. Cable television

15. Utilities

16. New cell phone

17. Groceries

18. Housing

19. The latest in fashion

20. Transportation

Short Answer

21. Have you ever purchased something and then felt guilty afterward? Explain.

22. How does advertising affect your buying decisions?

23. Describe the five steps to follow before making a significant purchase.

24. Differentiate between a want and a need.

25. Why do so many people fall for financing as a marketing tool? Describe a financing offer that you have recently seen or heard about.

Case Studies

26. Brett and Emily want to buy a new couch and have found the one they want for $999. They only have $200 saved, but they can take advantage of a six month same-as-cash deal. Over the next six months, they could save up the extra $799, pay it off early, and save on the interest. Is this a good idea? What advice would you give them?

27. Dan is at Excellent Electronics looking at plasma televisions when he is approached by a salesperson. After hearing about the current store offer of no interest for one year, Dan decides that he should purchase the television and take advantage of this free money while it is available. He charges the entire purchase, which totals $1,164.94 (including tax). What should Dan's monthly payments be if he intends to pay off the television in full before the year is up? Dan misses the last payment by two days and now has to pay the interest charges for the entire year. If the APR is 22.9%, how much does he owe for the accrued interest? What does Dan learn about using other people's money?

28. Sherry wants to buy a car but only has an extra $275 per month in her budget. She has found a dealer that will lease her a nice car for $225 per month over four years. She is excited because she is getting a nice car, but she is also saving $50 per month in payments. What would Dave say to Sherry?

CREDIT BUREAUS and COLLECTION PRACTICES

What do other high school students know about credit bureaus and collection practices?

Bad decisions lead to bad debt and bad credit. We asked some high school students if they or someone they knew ever bought something they couldn't afford:

> "My friends bought an ATV and I thought I had to get one, too. **I thought I'd be able to pay for it, but I lost my job and then my ATV.**"
>
> Senior, Georgia

"I know someone who bought a dirt bike that he couldn't afford. He had to get a job, quit football and work after school everyday in order to make the payments."

Senior, Alabama

"A friend of my dad used a credit card to buy something he couldn't afford. When the creditors began calling, the family stopped answering their phone and ended up asking my dad to help pay off the debt."

Senior, Texas

"My neighbor bought a car he couldn't afford and it got repossessed."

Junior, Missouri

"Some people I know bought a bunch of stuff they didn't need, like video games, a pool table, etc. They got into debt and had to file for bankruptcy."

Sophomore, Tennessee

LEARNING OUTCOMES

Evaluate the myth of building your credit score.

Describe precautions that will protect you from identity theft.

Explain how to correct inaccuracies on a credit report.

Become familiar with the Federal Fair Debt Collection Practices Act and parameters regulating collectors.

KEY TERMS

Bankruptcy
Credit Bureau
Credit Report
Chapter 7 Bankruptcy
Garnishment
Pro-Rata

What do you know about credit bureaus and collection practices?

Answer the following questions before you watch the lesson. At the completion of the lesson, review the questions again to see if your views changed.

Before			After	
True	False		True	False
☐	☐	1. The collection industry is a lucrative business, producing over $40 billion a year in revenues from fees paid to collectors.	☐	☐
☐	☐	2. Collectors can buy debt for as little as 25 cents for each $100 in face value, making a huge profit.	☐	☐
☐	☐	3. A person that owes debt has few legal protections and should receive multiple calls at work and home, which are unpleasant in nature.	☐	☐
☐	☐	4. Your FICO score is important and you should strive to get the highest score you possibly can as it is an indicator of responsible money management.	☐	☐
☐	☐	5. More than 75% of credit reports contain mistakes of some sort.	☐	☐
☐	☐	6. Collectors generally follow the guidelines set forth in the Fair Debt Collection Practices Act, which gives consumers only a few legal rights.	☐	☐
☐	☐	7. Consumers are entitled to sue a debt collector if they violate the Fair Debt Collection Practices Act.	☐	☐
☐	☐	8. When a collector tells you that they are going to garnish your wages immediately, you should make some type of payment to prevent this from happening.	☐	☐
☐	☐	9. Identity theft is the fastest-growing white collar crime in America.	☐	☐
☐	☐	10. If you are willing to pay a fee, you can have your credit cleaned up, which will improve your FICO score.	☐	☐

Credit Score

One More Myth

▶ MYTH: You need to take out a credit card or car loan to "build up your _____ _____."

▶ TRUTH: The _____ score is an "I love _____" score and is not a measure of winning financially.

◀ END OF VIDEO PART 1

Credit Bureaus

Account information is removed from your credit report _____ years after the last activity on the account, except for a Chapter 7 bankruptcy, which stays on for _____ years.

Beware of credit clean–up scams. The only information that may be legally removed from a credit report is _____ information.

✚ MORE INFO

FICO stands for Fair Isaac Corporation, which developed a score-based rating system that many companies use to measure an individual's credit risk. Although this measurement has become widely accepted, it is a faulty standard that is based on debt, not wealth.

Five Components of the FICO Score

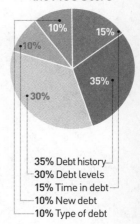

35% Debt history
30% Debt levels
15% Time in debt
10% New debt
10% Type of debt

www.myfico.com

WISE GUYS

"I've never been poor, only broke. Being poor is a frame of mind. Being broke is only a temporary position."

Mike Todd

Correcting Credit Report Inaccuracies

The National Association of State Public Interest Research Groups (U.S. PIRG) did a survey of 200 adults in 30 states who checked their credit report for accuracy.

▶ _____ of those credit reports contained mistakes of some sort and _____ of them contained errors serious enough to result in the denial of credit.

▶ _____ of the credit reports contained credit accounts that had been closed by the consumer but incorrectly remained listed as open.

"Why do I need to worry about learning this finance stuff? I live at home and my parents pay for everything."

DAVE'S ANSWER: You're in school and will be out on your own in just a few years. Now is the time to build great financial habits. Correcting poor habits gets harder and harder as you grow older. If you don't believe me, take a look around. Seventy percent of Americans live paycheck-to-paycheck according to *The Wall Street Journal*. They spend everything they make and then they're broke again until the next paycheck comes around. That means these people are one emergency away from financial disaster. Worse yet, many of them know it and refuse to do anything about it. Why? They've developed poor financial habits and choose not to correct them.

From now through college, you should be working to establish really good personal habits in all areas, not just financial. You're building character to become a mature, successful adult. Too many people just party through this time and put off growing up until it's too late. Suddenly they find themselves out on their own with other people—like a spouse or children— depending on them to survive, but they don't have the skills to succeed. This is not a plan. Don't play that game!

▶ _____ listed the same mortgage or loan twice.

You should check your credit report _____, which you can now do for free.

The three credit bureaus are Experian, TransUnion, and Equifax.

Identity Theft: What to Do

Identity theft is the fastest-growing _____ _____ crime in North America today.

1. Place a _____ _____ alert on your credit bureau report (stays on for 90 days without a police report).

2. Get a _____ _____.

   80% of identities are stolen by people you know.

3. Remember, this is_____. You owe _____ and should pay _____.

4. Contact the_____ _____ division of each creditor and furnish _____.

5. Be _____, this will take some time. You now have a new _____.

$ MONEY FACTS

States with the highest per capita rates of ID theft:
- Arizona
- Nevada
- California
- Texas
- Florida
- Colorado
- Georgia
- New York

States with the lowest per capita rates of ID theft:
- Montana
- Wisconsin
- Wyoming
- Kentucky
- Maine
- West Virginia
- Iowa
- South Dakota
- North Dakota
- Vermont

Federal Trade Commission

✚ MORE INFO

Of all the identity theft victims who call in to *The Dave Ramsey Show*, approximately half of them know the person who stole their identity. The thief is often a friend or family member.

REAL LIFE

Young people seem to have little to lose from identity theft, which makes them easy targets. College students are particularly vulnerable to identity theft. In fact, people aged 18-29 are the most commonly victimized age group when it comes to this white collar crime.

A young listener wrote this letter to *The Dave Ramsey Show:*

"My third day of college, I applied for several credit cards on campus. Five years later, I found out that my personal information was posted on a web site. I had cars bought in my name and credit accounts across the country. A college student who ran one of the credit card booths was responsible for posting my information. Even though I now have a new Social Security number, I constantly have to monitor my credit reports. I have had to explain all of this to employers who run background checks on me. Those free T-shirts wound up costing me $150,000!"

Obviously, you're never too young to be careful with your personal information. Here are some tips to protect yourself from identity theft:
- Use a paper shredder and destroy credit card offers and mail.
- Check your credit reports annually.
- Never print your Social Security number or drivers license number on your checks.
- Sign the back of your debit card and write "PHOTO ID REQUIRED."
- Create strong passwords using a combination of letters, characters, and numbers.
- Keep passwords and personal information confidential.

An updated version of the 1977 Federal Fair Credit Reporting Act (FFCRA) requires a credit bureau to _____ all inaccuracies within _____ days of notification of such inaccuracies.

To clean your credit report of inaccurate information, take the following steps:

1. Write a separate letter for each inaccuracy.

2. Staple a copy of your credit report to each letter.

3. Circle the account number.

NOTE: You should also request that "inquiries" be removed. All of these letters should be sent _____ mail with return receipt requested to prove when they receive the letter. If the credit bureau does not prove the accuracy of the account within _____ days, request that they remove the _____ account from your file.

You will have to be assertive after the 30-day period.

Lodge any _____ with the Federal Trade Commission and your state's Consumer Affairs Division.

> END OF VIDEO PART 2

$ MONEY FACTS

People age 18–29 are the **number one** target of identity thieves.

Quest Communications

68% of teens report they are concerned about online identity theft and fraud.

Charles Schwab Survey

23% of teens know what a credit score is.

Charles Schwab Survey

Collection Practices

The best way to pay debt is with a _____.

A collector's job is not to help your overall situation. His only job is to get your _____.

Collectors are trained _____ or _____.

They are typically low-paid positions with high _____.

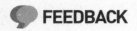

FEEDBACK

Identity thieves and scammers work in clever ways. Have you ever been scammed on the phone or internet?

"Someone created a phishing site that had 'myspace' in the domain so I logged in and they stole all of my info."

Senior, Texas

"I was taking a quiz on the internet and all of a sudden it asked for my cell phone number. Stupidly I gave it to them and the company started charging $9.99 a month to my cell phone."

Sophomore, Florida

"One time a fake phone book company called to confirm the information for my family's business. They asked if I wanted to extend the listing for 'two more years for $399,' and I said yes, thinking it was $3.99. The bill we received in the mail was for $399 and we paid it because they said it was already printed. But it was not a real company and we have nothing to show for our money."

Senior, Texas

They are taught in their training to evoke strong

_____.

The way to counteract this technique is to ALWAYS pay _____ first, and then you set the order of payment.

Always set your priorities by the Four Walls:

1. Food
2. Shelter
3. Clothing
4. Transportation

> END OF VIDEO PART 3

Federal Fair Debt Collections Practices Act

In 1977, a consumer law was passed by Congress called the Federal Fair Debt Collection Practices Act (FFDCPA) to protect you from unfair collectors. The law technically only applies to collection agencies (not your creditor), but later court cases make most creditors also abide by the FFDCPA.

> ▶ The Act states that _____ is illegal, and restricts a collector's calls between the hours of _____ and _____ (unless they have your permission).

> ▶ The Act also allows you to demand that a creditor cease calling you at _____. You should request this in writing by _____ _____ with return receipt requested.

- The Act even allows you to insist that a creditor stop _____ contact except to notify you of _____ proceedings. This is called a cease-and-desist letter.

- Do not use a cease-and-desist letter except in horrible situations, because all _____ stop and any hope of a positive resolution is lost.

- No collector or creditor may _____ a bank account or _____ wages without proper and lengthy court action, except in the case of delinquent IRS or student loan debt. All such threats are a bluff.

$ MONEY FACTS

The **number one** consumer complaint the Federal Trade Commission receives is regarding **debt collectors.**

Federal Trade Commission

Pro Rata Plan

Your plan should include as much prompt repayment of debt as possible, but YOU must set your priorities of repayment.

DO NOT let a collector use your _____ _____ as a paper club. ◀ END OF VIDEO PART 4

When you are unable to pay the minimum payments, use the _____ _____ plan.

Pro Rata Debt List

"Pro rata" means the fair share, or the percent of your total debt each creditor represents. This will determine how much you should send them when you cannot make the minimum payments. Even if you cannot pay your creditors what they request, you should pay everyone as much as you can. Send the check for their pro rata share, along with a copy of your budget and this form, every month. Do this even if the creditor says they will not accept it.

Do you need to use the pro rata plan?

First, use your monthly cash flow plan to determine your total disposable income. Simply write down your income on the line at the top of the form. Then, write down the total you spend on necessities (not including consumer debt) each month. Subtract the necessity expense from the income, and you are left with your disposable income. This is the money you have to put toward your debts.

Second, add up your total amount of debt, not including your home, and write that in the blank provided. Below that, write in the total of the minimum monthly payments on all your debts. If the total of your minimum payments is greater than your total disposable income, you need to use the pro rata plan.

For example, Joe and Suzie have a total debt of $2,000, with a combined total minimum payment of $310. However, this family only has $200 in disposable income each month, which means they do not have enough money to make the minimum payments. So, they will use the pro rata plan to give each creditor their fair share of the family's $200.

How to Use This Form

This form has six columns:
1. Item: the name and type of the account.
2. Total Payoff: the total amount due on the account.
3. Total Debt: the combined total of all your debts.
4. Percent: the portion of the total debt load that each account represents. You can calculate this by simply dividing the Total Payoff by the Total Debt for each line.
5. Disposable Income: the amount of money you have left after paying necessities.
6. New Payment: the amount that you will now send to each creditor. You calculate this by multiplying the numbers in each line's Percent and Disposable Income columns.

The pro rata plan helps you to meet your obligations to the best of your ability. Of course, your creditors will not like receiving less than their required minimum payments. However, if you keep sending them checks, they'll most likely keep cashing them.

Pro Rata Debt List (Continued)

Income $3361

Necessity Expense   – $3161

Disposable Income   = $200

Total Debt: $2,000

Total Monthly Payments: $310

ITEM	TOTAL PAYOFF		TOTAL / DEBT		= PERCENT	DISPOSABLE X INCOME		= NEW PAYMENT
JC Penney	100	/	2,000	=	5% (.05)	X	200	= $10
Sears	200	/	2,000	=	10% (.10)	X	200	= $20
MBNA Visa	200	/	2,000	=	10% (.10)	X	200	= $20
Citibank Visa	300	/	2,000	=	15% (.15)	X	200	= $30
Discover	1,200	/	2,000	=	60% (.60)	X	200	= $120
		/		=		X		=
		/		=		X		=
		/		=		X		=
		/		=		X		=
		/		=		X		=
		/		=		X		=
		/		=		X		=
		/		=		X		=
		/		=		X		=
		/		=		X		=
		/		=		X		=
		/		=		X		=
		/		=		X		=
		/		=		X		=

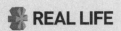 **REAL LIFE**

Borrowing money and failing to pay it back has some serious consequences. Here are some terms commonly used when dealing with debt problems that have gone too far. This is lingo you don't want to experience first hand.

Foreclosure—Process by which the holder of a mortgage sells the property of a homeowner who has not made interest and/or principal payments on time as stipulated in the mortgage contract.

Repossession—Think of the "Repo Man." Repossession is taking something back (like a car) for failure to make payments.

Bankruptcy—A legal procedure for dealing with debt problems of individuals and businesses.

Garnishment—A court-ordered attachment that allows a lender to take monies owed directly from a borrower's paycheck; only allowed as part of a court judgement.

Surrender of Collateral—In a bankruptcy proceeding, a debtor can give up property (collateral) to the creditor in exchange for a clean slate.

Delinquency—Broadly refers to a borrower not being current on his or her payments.

Lawsuits

Eventually, if you are making no payments and have cut no deals, you will get sued.

Typically, lawsuits for under _____ are filed in General Sessions Court (or small claims court), which is a fairly informal proceeding.

Before you are sued, you will be served by the local sheriff's department and typically given _____ days notice of the court date.

In court, if the debt is valid, even if you fight, you will _____. From that date you will generally have 30 days before the _____ becomes final and _____ or attachments begin.

"My older sister has run up some pretty large debts and a creditor somehow got our parent's phone number. Now this company is calling my parents four or five times a day, thinking that if they're pushy enough they'll pay them. What can they do?"

DAVE'S ANSWER: First, your mom and dad should get an answering machine—one that has a memo button that allows them to record conversations. The next time these bozos call, your parents should get on the phone and explain to them that the conversation is being recorded and that they are not liable for your sister's debt. Let them know, too, that if they ever contact them again about this matter that they will sue!

Your parents also need to tell them that if they call them again, they will file a complaint with the Federal Trade Commission. What this company is doing is a violation of federal law and the Federal Fair Debt Collections Practices Act. If the caller can't understand that, make them put a supervisor on the line and repeat it. Your dad needs to crawl all over these people, because what they're doing is illegal, immoral and just plain mean!

Even if he did owe the bill, calling that many times a day is still a violation of federal law. He's not going to get rid of these people by being nice!

AT ANY TIME during the process, you may settle with the creditor or their attorney in writing. If you are not able to reach an agreement, you can file with the court a "_____ _____ motion," called a "pauper's oath" in some states.

- ▶ If you're going to settle, get it in writing
- ▶ Never give electronic access to your checking account
- ▶ Never give post-dated checks   **END OF VIDEO PART 5**

$ MONEY FACTS

40% of Americans, under the age of 25, believe they are more likely to be hit by lightning, to be audited by the IRS, or to win the lottery than be the victim of a computer security problem.

National Cyber Security Alliance

Sit back. Relax. Put your pencil down. There are no fill-in-the-blanks in part six of this chapter. ◀ END OF VIDEO PART 6

Recap and Review

Identity theft is on the rise! Be careful with your personal information, including drivers license, Social Security number, account numbers, phone numbers, addresses and passwords.

Do not fall for the "I have to build up my credit score" myth. Your FICO score is an "I love debt" score.

Check your credit bureau report annually.

The Federal Fair Debt Collection Practices Act sets up restrictions that creditors must follow.

Always set your priorities by the Four Walls: food, shelter, clothing and transportation.

Credit Bureaus

The FACT Act amendments to the Fair Credit Reporting Act require the nationwide credit bureaus to provide consumers, upon request, one free personal credit report in any 12-month period. You may contact the Central Source online at www.annualcreditreport.com or by calling toll free (877) FACT ACT. Free copies are also available if you have been denied credit in the past 60 days and the creditor used their services.

EXPERIAN

(888) 397-3742

www.experian.com

EQUIFAX CREDIT BUREAU

(800) 685-1111

www.equifax.com

TRANSUNION CREDIT BUREAU

(877) 322-8228

www.transunion.com

FEDERAL TRADE COMMISSION

Publishes a brief, semi-annual list (March and September) on card pricing by the largest issuers for $5 per copy. Offers a number of free credit-related publications.

(202) 326-2222

600 Pennsylvania Avenue, N.W. Washington, D.C. 20580

www.ftc.gov

Be Proactive

Decrease unauthorized direct mail marketing (including pre-approved credit card offers) and unwanted telemarketing calls!

PRE-SCREENING OPT OUT

Phone:(888) 567-8688

www.optoutprescreen.com

NATIONAL DO NOT CALL REGISTRY

Phone:(888) 382-1222

www.donotcall.gov

You can write a letter and request to be removed from direct marketing databases for five years. Be sure to include your name, home phone number, address, and your signature. If your address changes, you must make another request.

FOR DIRECT MAILINGS:

Mail Preference Service
Direct Marketing Association
P.O. Box 282
Carmel, NY 10512

www.dmachoice.org

FOR TELEMARKETING:

Telephone Preference Service
Direct Marketing Association
P.O. Box 1559
Carmel, NY 10512

www.dmachoice.org

Vocabulary

Bankruptcy
Credit Bureau
Credit Report
Chapter 7 Bankruptcy
Disposable Income
FFDCPA
FFCRA
Fraud
Garnishment
Necessities
Pro Rata

Matching

a. FICO score
b. collectors
c. garnishment
d. pro rata
e. Four Walls
f. identity theft
g. credit bureau
h. FFDCPA
i. fraud

___ 1. Gives creditors a "fair share"

___ 2. "I love debt" score

___ 3. Using another person's information to obtain goods or services

___ 4. TransUnion

___ 5. Court order allowing a lender to take money directly from the debtor's paycheck

___ 6. Trained salespeople or telemarketers

___ 7. Food, shelter, clothing, transportation

True or False

Determine whether these statements are true or false. Change the false statements to read true.

_____ 8. You should always pay the collectors first.

_____

_____

_____

_____ 9. The best way to deal with debt is with a plan.

_____

_____

_____

_____ 10. The Federal Fair Debt Collection Practices Act allows creditors to call between 7 a.m. and 10 p.m.

_____

_____

_____

_____ 11. If you are a victim of identity theft, you are only responsible for the first $250 of debt.

_____

_____

_____

_____ 12. You should check your credit report every year.

_____

_____

_____

Multiple Choice

13. Passed in 1977 to protect you from unfair collectors:
    a. FDIC
    b. FHA
    c. FFDCPA
    d. FFCRA

14. Which of the following is one of the Four Walls:
    a. cable television
    b. mortgage payment
    c. cell phone bill
    d. designer jeans

15. It is a good idea to check your credit report:
    a. every six months
    b. every three years
    c. every year
    d. every five years

16. Which of the following tactics are collectors likely to use?
    a. lying
    b. harassment
    c. being friendly
    d. all of the above

17. Which of the following is not a way to build your FICO score?
    a. pay cash for all purchases
    b. get a personal loan from the bank
    c. sign up and use credit cards
    d. all of the above

18. Which piece of information, if stolen, is not likely to lead to identity theft?
    a. drivers license
    b. phone number
    c. credit card number
    d. Social Security number

19. The pro rata payment includes which of the following elements:
    a. repayment of debt as soon as possible
    b. using the Four Walls to set priorities
    c. giving a percentage of debt to each creditor
    d. all of the above

20. The fastest growing group of people filing for bankruptcy are:
    a. under 25
    b. 25-30
    c. 30-45
    d. senior citizens

Short Answer

21. What is the best way to deal with collectors?

22. Explain the steps to take if you find an error on your credit report.

23. List some precautions to take to help safeguard against identity theft.

24. Describe some common tactics used by collectors. Why do they use these?

25. Refute the myth, "I need to build my credit score."

Case Studies

26. Aaron and Hannah are late making their payments and collectors are beginning to call daily. They are threatening to garnish their wages over the credit card debt amounting to $13,000. Their car is about to be repossessed because they haven't made the payment in 3 months. Aaron and Hannah both work and are considering part-time jobs to catch up. They have a 16-year-old son who plays sports, so they would have to miss his games. The collectors are getting more and more abusive with every call. What advice would Dave give Aaron and Hannah? Devise a plan for them to follow, including how to deal with the collectors.

27. Chelsea is behind on her credit card and car payments. One collector has been calling her at work and threatening to garnish her wages if she doesn't find a way to get current. Chelsea recently began listening to Dave Ramsey and does have a financial plan to take care of the problem. However, she is now terrified and is considering not making her mortgage payment to get this collector to stop calling. Use what you learned in this lesson to help Chelsea deal with this collector and stick to her financial plan.

28. Neal recently received a call from the bank telling him that he was late making payments on his loan. Neal does not have a loan with that or any other bank, as he lives debt free. What problem does Neal most likely have and what steps does he need to take to correct it?

UNIT 3
FINANCIAL RESPONSIBILITY
and MONEY MANAGEMENT

What do other high school students know about budgeting?

We asked high school students to share some tips on how to handle their money:

> "Put yourself on a budget and **be wise with your money.** That way you won't be tempted to dip into your savings account.
>
> Freshman, Florida

"Expenses don't just happen, they're always there. It takes practice to save money and not spend it all."

Junior, Utah

"Get direct deposit and put money right into your savings account. Then, only spend the money you have left over."

Senior, Missouri

"It is a good idea to start saving with your first pay check because once you start spending, it is hard to stop."

Junior, Tennessee

"It is good to make a money plan. You should save a percentage every month, even if it is not a lot."

Freshman, Texas

LEARNING OUTCOMES

Explain how money is active.

Analyze reasons why people do not do a budget.

Examine common problems associated with budget failures.

Explain the benefits of a budget.

Demonstrate how to complete a zero-based budget.

KEY TERMS

Budget
Discipline
Envelope System
Impulse Purchase
Reconcile
Zero-Based Budget

BEFORE YOU BEGIN

What do you know about budgeting?

How do you rate compared to other young adults? Take the following survey and see how close you and your classmates line up with the ideas and values that other teens have about money.

Agree	Disagree	
☐	☐	1. It is important to know how to live within my means and have good money habits to be successful in life.
☐	☐	2. I expect and would like my parents to stop supporting me before age 25.
☐	☐	3. I am knowledgeable about money management, including budgeting and saving.
☐	☐	4. I am prepared to deal with the adult financial world after school.
☐	☐	5. I know how to budget my money.
☐	☐	6. I know how to balance a checkbook and reconcile an account register to a bank statement.
☐	☐	7. I know how to write a check.
☐	☐	8. I have more than $100 in savings.

On average, I spend $_____ per week.

My top three monthly expenses are:

1. ....

2. ....

3. ....

Cash Flow Planning

Money is _____.

You must do a written _____ _____
plan every _____. `END OF VIDEO PART 1`

You must also keep your checkbook _____.

_____ are a sign of crisis living and sloppy,
lazy _____ habits.

Use _____ checks if necessary.

If not managed and made to behave, the _____ card and
the _____ card are certain to become budget busters.

Reasons We Don't Do a Cash Flow Plan

Most people hate the word "budget" for four reasons:

1. It has a _____ _____ connotation.

2. It has been used to _____ them.

3. They've never had a budget that _____.

4. Paralysis from _____ of what they
   will find. `END OF VIDEO PART 2`

MONEY FACTS

54% of those that do a poor job of sticking to a budget claim "unexpected expenses" as the reason.

bankrate.com

93% of teens say it's important to know how to live within your means.

Charles Schwab Survey

MORE INFO

It's important to know how much things cost before you buy. Whether it's a vacation, a car with all the options, or a house, you need to know the total price. A smart doctor once wrote, "Suppose one of you wants to build a tower. What is the first thing you will do? Won't you sit down and figure out how much it will cost and if you have enough money? What if you start building the tower, but cannot finish? Everyone who sees what is happening will laugh. They will say, 'You started building, but could not finish the job.'" (Luke 14:28-30)

⊕ MORE INFO

Your budget will only work if you follow it. Here are three tips to help you stick to a budget.

WRITE IT DOWN
A budget is not a form of medieval torture! It is YOUR game plan, where YOU tell YOUR money what YOU want it to do. This isn't rocket science! Just give every dollar a name on paper.

STAY AWAY FROM PLACES THAT TEMPT YOU TO SPEND
If you have a problem sticking to a budget, you may not yet be disciplined. If that's the case, stay out of the mall or wherever your spending weakness occurs. Think of it like this: it's not smart for an alcoholic to hang out at a bar.

USE THE ENVELOPE SYSTEM
Take some envelopes, write the budget categories on the envelopes, and use only that money to purchase those items. Try only a couple of categories at first until you get the hang of it. If the money is not in there, you can't spend it. Easy as pie. And remember, it takes practice; you won't get it right the first time.

Cash flow plans do not work when you:

1. _____ things _____.

2. _____ your plan.

3. Don't actually _____ _____.

4. Don't actually _____ on it.

Reasons We Should Do a Cash Flow Plan

A written plan removes the "management by _____" from your finances.

_____money goes farther.

A written plan, if actually lived and agreed on, will remove many of the _____ _____ from your marriage.

A written plan, if actually lived and agreed on, will remove much of the _____,_____, and _____ that may be part of buying necessities such as food or clothing.

A written plan, if actually lived and agreed on, will remove many of the _____ from your life, consequently removing a lot of _____.

A written plan, if actually lived and agreed on, will show if you are _____ on a certain area.

How To Balance Your Checking Account

Keep your account register current by subtracting checks, debit card purchases and withdrawals. Then add deposits as they're made to keep your account balanced correctly.

Balance your checking account within 72 hours of receiving your bank statement or go online once a month to review your account and make sure there aren't any mistakes.

What do I need to balance my account?

1. Your account register
2. Your last bank statement (in print or online)
3. A reconciliation sheet (located on the back of most statements)

Where do I start?

Start by putting check marks in your register for each of the checks, debit card purchases and other withdrawals, as well as deposits included in your bank statement. Make an entry in your register for any bank service charges or interest paid.

On the reconciliation sheet, list any outstanding checks, withdrawals or other deductions that are in your register that are not on your bank statement and total the list.

On the reconciliation sheet, list any deposits that are in your register but are not included on your bank statement. Total the list.

Beginning with the ending balance from your bank statement, subtract the total withdrawals and add the total deposits that were not on your statement.

Compare with your register balance. If they don't agree, double check your lists and re-add your register entries until you find the difference. If the numbers will not agree, you're probably missing a transaction in your register. Make sure every transaction on your statement has been recorded and try again. In some cases, you may need your bank's help in getting your register to balance if you haven't done it in a while.

Checking Account Register

Check Number	Date	Fee	Transaction Description	Payment	Deposit	Balance
						$564.46
5671	8/12	✗	One Stop Grocery	57.40		507.06
5672	8/14		Electric Company	101.00		406.06
	8/14		Paycheck		700.00	1106.06
5673	8/16		Telephone Company	50.00		1056.06
5674	8/19		One Stop Grocery	66.00		990.06
		✗	Bank Service Charge	2.50		987.56

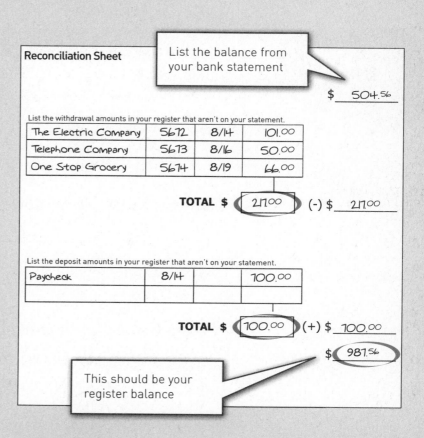

Reconciliation Sheet

List the balance from your bank statement

$ 504.56

List the withdrawal amounts in your register that aren't on your statement.

The Electric Company	5672	8/14	101.00
Telephone Company	5673	8/16	50.00
One Stop Grocery	5674	8/19	66.00

TOTAL $ 217.00 (-) $ 217.00

List the deposit amounts in your register that aren't on your statement.

| Paycheck | 8/14 | | 100.00 |
| | | | |

TOTAL $ 100.00 (+) $ 100.00

$ 987.56

This should be your register balance

"My mom and dad are trying to teach me how to keep a checkbook in order. Why is this so hard?"

DAVE'S ANSWER: It's really not that hard. Keeping a checkbook in order is simple addition and subtraction. The problem most people seem to have is remembering to write everything down in it. Let's say you start out with $100. If you spend $20, you have $80 left, right? But when people forget to write down the money they spend, it throws everything off, and you end up thinking you have more money than you really do.

Just take a few seconds and write it down right after you buy something. It may take a little time, but it's better than running out of money and getting nasty notes from the bank!

"I just got a part-time job, and I want to make sure I save some money in case something bad happens to my car. Do you think I should tell my parents I want to open a checking account AND a savings account?"

DAVE'S ANSWER: First, congratulations on the new job! You've taken a big first step toward financial independence.

Second, I think it's a great idea to keep your checking and saving accounts separate, and here's why. If you put all your money in one place, it becomes too easy to dip into your savings or emergency fund when you're writing checks. This defeats the original purpose of saving money.

This separation acts as a mental note and a barrier. It's a way of telling you that you've reached your spending limit!

The easiest and most powerful plan is a _____-based plan using the _____ system.

END OF VIDEO PART 3

There are no fill-in-the-blanks for parts 4-6. Turn to the forms beginning on page 100 to follow along with Dave.

How do you budget with irregular income?

First, make a list of all of your expenses for the month ahead. Write down absolutely everything that you'll need or want to spend money on. This includes everything from rent to gas to savings to weekend fun money. Write it all down.

Then, prioritize the list in order of importance. Ask yourself, "If I only have enough to pay for one thing, what would it be?" That's number one. Then ask, "If I only have enough to pay for one more thing, what would it be?" That's number two. Keep that up all the way down the list.

Now, you're ready to get paid! When your check comes in, just spend your money all the way down the list. When the money's gone, you're done spending for the month. That's why it is so important to prioritize the list. You may not have enough cash for everything you want to do each month, so make sure you're making the best with what you have.

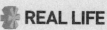**REAL LIFE**

Shaun sells real estate and has what we call an "irregular income." That just means his income fluctuates from month to month. If you're in this situation, you absolutely must do a monthly budget, but you'll do it a little differently.

Review and Recap

Do a written budget! You have to tell your money what to do.

Spend every dollar on paper before the month begins.

Use the envelope system and fill each envelope with the money allotted to that category.

When it's gone, you are done spending for that category—no ATM visits!

Give it time. It takes 3-4 months to get it right.

! STUPID TAX

"I deposited my check at an ATM and went shopping the next day. My debit card was declined at the register and it was really embarrassing. I finally figured out that you shouldn't deposit money on a Saturday because banks are closed Sunday and the check won't post."

Senior, Missouri

"I overdrew my checking account one time because I wrote down an amount incorrectly. The bank was going to charge me over $50 in fees for my $3.36 error."

Senior, Alabama

Major Components of a Healthy Financial Plan

	ACTION NEEDED	ACTION DATE
Written Cash Flow Plan	Complete first budget	NOW!
Will and/or Estate Plan	Make an appt. with lawyer	June 6
Debt Reduction Plan	Begin debt snowball	July 1
Tax Reduction Plan	NA	NA
Emergency Funding	On hold until Baby Step 3	NA
Retirement Funding	On hold until Baby Step 4	NA
College Funding	On hold until Baby Step 5	NA
Charitable Giving	Start giving	June 15
Teach My Children	Get Financial Peace Jr.	August
Life Insurance	Done	NA
Health Insurance	Done	NA
Disability Insurance	Check company options	This week
Auto Insurance	Check current policy details	July 1
Homeowner's Insurance	Check replacement cost	This week

I ___Joe & Suzie Public___, a responsible adult, do hereby promise to take the above stated actions by the above stated dates to financially secure the well-being of my (our) family and myself (ourselves).

Signed: ___Joe Q. Public___ Date: ___June 2___

Signed: ___Suzie Q. Public___ Date: ___June 2___

Consumer Equity Sheet

ITEM / DESCRIBE	VALUE	-DEBT	=EQUITY
Real Estate _____	$180,000	$149,000	$31,000
Real Estate _____			
Car _____	$2,500		$2,500
Car _____	$3,000		$3,000
Cash On Hand			
Checking Account			
Checking Account			
Savings Account	$1,600		$1,600
Money Market Account			
Mutual Funds			
Retirement Plan 1	$400		$400
Retirement Plan 2	$8,000		$8,000
Cash Value (Insurance)			
Household Items	$30,000		$30,000
Jewelry			
Antiques			
Boat			
Unsecured Debt (Neg)			
Credit Card Debt (Neg)			
Other _____			
Other _____			
Other _____			
TOTAL	$225,500	$149,000	$76,500

Income Sources

SOURCE	AMOUNT	PERIOD/DESCRIBE
Salary 1	$2,716	1st of Month
Salary 2	$945	1st & 15th – $472.50
Salary 3		
Bonus		
Self-Employment		
Interest Income		
Dividend Income		
Royalty Income		
Rents		
Notes		
Alimony		
Child Support		
AFDC		
Unemployment		
Social Security		
Pension		
Annuity		
Disability Income		
Cash Gifts		
Trust Fund		
Other_____		
Other_____		
Other_____		
TOTAL	$3,661	

Lump Sum Payment Planning

Payments you make on a non-monthly basis, such as insurance premiums and taxes, can be budget busters if you do not plan for them every month. Therefore, you must annualize the cost and convert these to monthly budget items. That way, you can save the money each month and will not be caught off-guard when your bi-monthly, quarterly, semi-annual, or annual bills come due. Simply divide the annual cost by 12 to determine the monthly amount you should save for each item.

ITEM NEEDED	ANNUAL AMOUNT		MONTHLY AMOUNT
Real Estate Taxes		/ 12 =	
Homeowner's Insurance		/ 12 =	
Home Repairs	$1,800	/ 12 =	$150
Replace Furniture		/ 12 =	
Medical Bills	$600	/ 12 =	$50
Health Insurance		/ 12 =	
Life Insurance		/ 12 =	
Disability Insurance		/ 12 =	
Car Insurance		/ 12 =	
Car Repair/Tags		/ 12 =	
Replace Car		/ 12 =	
Clothing		/ 12 =	
Tuition		/ 12 =	
Bank Note		/ 12 =	
IRS (Self-Employed)		/ 12 =	
Vacation	$1,200	/ 12 =	$100
Gifts (including Christmas)		/ 12 =	
Other _____		/ 12 =	

Monthly Cash Flow Plan

Every single dollar of your income should be allocated to some category on this form. When you're done, your total income minus expenses should equal zero. If it doesn't, then you need to adjust some categories (such as debt reduction, giving, or saving) so that it does equal zero. Use some common sense here, too. Do not leave things like clothes, car repairs, or home improvements off this list. If you don't plan for these things, then you're only setting yourself up for failure later.

Yes, this budget form is long. It's *really* long. (Pages 104-107.) We do that so that we can list practically every expense imaginable on this form to prevent you from forgetting something. Don't expect to put something on every line item. Just use the ones that are relevant to your specific situation.

Every main category on this form has subcategories. Fill in the monthly expense for each subcategory, and then write down the grand total for that category. Later, as you actually pay the bills and work through the month, use the "Actually Spent" column to record what you really spent in each area. If there is a substantial difference between what you budgeted and what you spent, then you'll need to readjust the budget to make up for the difference. If one category continually comes up over or short for two or three months, then you need to adjust the budgeted amount accordingly.

Use the "% Take Home Pay" column to record what percentage of your income actually goes to each category. Then, use the "Recommended Percentages" form to see if your percentages are in line with what we recommend.

Notes:

- An asterisk (*) beside an item indicates an area for which you should use the envelope system.

- The emergency fund should get all the savings until you've completed your full emergency fund of three to six months of expenses (Baby Step 3).

- Don't forget to include your annualized items from the "Lump Sum Payment Planning" form, including your Christmas gift planning.

Monthly Cash Flow Plan (Continued)

BUDGETED ITEM	SUB TOTAL	TOTAL	ACTUALLY SPENT	% OF TAKE HOME PAY
CHARITABLE GIFTS		$366		10%
SAVING				
Emergency Fund	$224			
Retirement Fund				
College Fund		$224		6%
HOUSING				
First Mortgage	$915			
Second Mortgage				
Real Estate Taxes				
Homeowner's Ins.				
Repairs or Mn. Fee				
Replace Furniture	$50			
Other _____		$965		27%
UTILITIES				
Electricity	$100			
Water	$55			
Gas	$75			
Phone	$45			
Trash				
Cable	$21	$296		8%
***FOOD**				
*Groceries	$360			
*Restaurants	$50	$410		12%
TRANSPORTATION				
Car Payment				
Car Payment				
*Gas and Oil	$150			
*Repairs and Tires				
Car Insurance	$80			
License and Taxes				
Car Replacement		$230		5%
PAGE 1 TOTAL		$2,491		

Monthly Cash Flow Plan (Continued)

BUDGETED ITEM	SUB TOTAL	TOTAL	ACTUALLY SPENT	% OF TAKE HOME PAY
*CLOTHING				
*Children				
*Adults	$100			
*Cleaning/Laundry		$100		3%
MEDICAL/HEALTH				
Disability Insurance				
Health Insurance	$300			
Doctor Bills	$50			
Dentist	$20			
Optometrist				
Medications		$370		10%
PERSONAL				
Life Insurance	$65			
Child Care				
*Baby Sitter				
*Toiletries				
*Cosmetics				
*Hair Care	$60			
Education/Adult				
School Tuition				
School Supplies				
Child Support				
Alimony				
Subscriptions				
Organization Dues	$25			
Gifts (incl. Christmas)				
Miscellaneous	$50			
*Blow Money	$100	$300		8%
PAGE 2 TOTAL		$770		

Monthly Cash Flow Plan (Continued)

BUDGETED ITEM	SUB TOTAL	TOTAL	ACTUALLY SPENT	% OF TAKE HOME PAY
RECREATION				
*Entertainment	$50			
Vacation	$25	$75		2%
DEBTS (Hopefully None)				
Visa 1	$100			
Visa 2				
Master Card 1	$75			
Master Card 2				
American Express	$50			
Discover Card				
Gas Card 1				
Gas Card 2				
Dept. Store Card 1				
Dept. Store Card 2				
Finance Co. 1				
Finance Co. 2				
Credit Line				
Student Loan 1	$100			
Student Loan 2				
Other _____				
Other _____				
Other _____				
Other _____				
Other _____		$325		9%
PAGE 3 TOTAL		$400		
PAGE 2 TOTAL		$770		
PAGE 1 TOTAL		$2,491		
GRAND TOTAL		$3,661		
TOTAL HOUSEHOLD INCOME		$3,661		
		ZERO		

Recommended Percentages

How much of your income should be spent on housing, giving, food, etc.? Through experience and research, we recommend the following percentages. However, you should remember that these are only recommended percentages. If you have an unusually high or low income, then these numbers could change dramatically. For example, if you have a high income, the percentage that is spent on food will be much lower than someone who earns half of that.

If you find that you spend much more in one category than we recommend, however, it may be necessary to adjust your lifestyle in that area in order to enjoy more freedom and flexibility across the board.

ITEM	ACTUAL %	RECOMMENDED %
Charitable Gifts	10%	10 – 15%
Saving	6%	5 – 10%
Housing	27%	25 – 35%
Utilities	8%	5 – 10%
Food	12%	5 – 15%
Transportation	5%	10 – 15%
Clothing	3%	2 – 7%
Medical/Health	10%	5 – 10%
Personal	8%	5 – 10%
Recreation	2%	5 – 10%
Debts	9%	5 – 10%

Allocated Spending Plan

Now that you've already planned out the entire month on the "Monthly Cash Flow Plan," let's get just a little bit more precise. On this form, you will allocate—or spend—all of your money from each individual pay period.

There are four columns on this form, representing the four weeks in a given month. You will use one column for each week you get paid. If you are married and your spouse earns an income, then you will both use this same form. For weeks in which you both receive a paycheck, simply add those two incomes together and use a single column. Be sure to write the pay date at the top of the column.

Now, go down the list and allocate each expense to a specific payday, using your bills' due dates as a guide. For example, if your phone bill is due on the 22nd and you get paid on the 15th and 30th, then you know that you would probably pay that bill from your income on the 15th. Some things, like utility bills, will be paid monthly, while other items, such as food and gasoline, could be weekly. The point here is to anticipate both your upcoming expenses and your upcoming income and plan accordingly.

Beside each line item, you'll see two blanks separated by a slash (/). Put the expense to the left of the slash and the remaining income from that pay period to the right of the slash. As you work your way down the column, the income remaining should diminish until you reach a perfect zero at the bottom of the list. If you have money left over at the end of the column, go back and adjust an area, such as savings or giving, so that you spend every single dollar.

This level of detail may be uncomfortable to you at first, but the payoff is worth it. By specifically "naming" every dollar before you actually get it in your hands, you will remove an incredible amount of stress and curb your overspending.

NOTES:

- If you have an irregular income, such as self-employment or commissions, you should use the "Irregular Income Planning" form instead of this "Allocated Spending Plan."

- If you know that you have an impulse spending problem, then you may want to allocate more money to the "Blow" category. That way, you are at least planning for it and setting up some boundaries for yourself.

- An asterisk (*) beside an item indicates an area for which you should use the envelope system.

Allocated Spending Plan (Continued)

PAY PERIOD:	7 / 1	7 / 8	7 / 15	7 / 22
ITEM:				
INCOME	$3,188	0	$472	0
CHARITABLE	366 / 2822	___ / ___	___ / ___	___ / ___
SAVING				
Emergency Fund	224 / 2598	___ / ___	___ / ___	___ / ___
Retirement Fund	___ / ___	___ / ___	___ / ___	___ / ___
College Fund	___ / ___	___ / ___	___ / ___	___ / ___
HOUSING				
First Mortgage	915 / 1683	___ / ___	___ / ___	___ / ___
Second Mortgage	___ / ___	___ / ___	___ / ___	___ / ___
Real Estate Taxes	___ / ___	___ / ___	___ / ___	___ / ___
Homeowner's Ins.	___ / ___	___ / ___	___ / ___	___ / ___
Repairs or Mn. Fees	___ / ___	___ / ___	___ / ___	___ / ___
Replace Furniture	___ / ___	___ / ___	50 / 422	___ / ___
Other _____	___ / ___	___ / ___	___ / ___	___ / ___
UTILITIES				
Electricity	100 / 1583	___ / ___	___ / ___	___ / ___
Water	___ / ___	___ / ___	55 / 367	___ / ___
Gas	___ / ___	___ / ___	75 / 292	___ / ___
Phone	45 / 1538	___ / ___	___ / ___	___ / ___
Trash	___ / ___	___ / ___	___ / ___	___ / ___
Cable	21 / 1517	___ / ___	___ / ___	___ / ___
*FOOD				
*Groceries	200 / 1317	___ / ___	160 / 132	___ / ___
*Restaurants	25 / 1292	___ / ___	25 / 107	___ / ___

Allocated Spending Plan (Continued)

TRANSPORTATION

Car Payment	____ / ____	____ / ____	____ / ____	____ / ____
Car Payment	____ / ____	____ / ____	____ / ____	____ / ____
*Gas and Oil	75 / 1217	____ / ____	75 / 32	____ / ____
*Repairs and Tires	____ / ____	____ / ____	____ / ____	____ / ____
Car Insurance	80 / 1137	____ / ____	____ / ____	____ / ____
License and Taxes	____ / ____	____ / ____	____ / ____	____ / ____
Car Replacement	____ / ____	____ / ____	____ / ____	____ / ____

*CLOTHING

*Children	____ / ____	____ / ____	____ / ____	____ / ____
*Adults	100 / 1037	____ / ____	____ / ____	____ / ____
*Cleaning/Laundry	____ / ____	____ / ____	____ / ____	____ / ____

MEDICAL/HEALTH

Disability Insurance	____ / ____	____ / ____	____ / ____	____ / ____
Health Insurance	300 / 737	____ / ____	____ / ____	____ / ____
Doctor	50 / 687	____ / ____	____ / ____	____ / ____
Dentist	____ / ____	____ / ____	20 / 12	____ / ____
Optometrist	____ / ____	____ / ____	____ / ____	____ / ____
Medications	____ / ____	____ / ____	____ / ____	____ / ____

PERSONAL

Life Insurance	65 / 622	____ / ____	____ / ____	____ / ____
Child Care	____ / ____	____ / ____	____ / ____	____ / ____
*Baby Sitter	____ / ____	____ / ____	____ / ____	____ / ____
*Toiletries	____ / ____	____ / ____	____ / ____	____ / ____
*Cosmetics	____ / ____	____ / ____	____ / ____	____ / ____
*Hair Care	____ / ____	____ / ____	____ / ____	____ / ____
Education/Adult	60 / 562	____ / ____	____ / ____	____ / ____
School Tuition	____ / ____	____ / ____	____ / ____	____ / ____
School Supplies	____ / ____	____ / ____	____ / ____	____ / ____
Child Support	____ / ____	____ / ____	____ / ____	____ / ____

Allocated Spending Plan (Continued)

Alimony	____ / ____	____ / ____	____ / ____	____ / ____
Subscriptions	____ / ____	____ / ____	____ / ____	____ / ____
Organization Dues	25 / 537	____ / ____	____ / ____	____ / ____
Gifts (including Christmas)	____ / ____	____ / ____	____ / ____	____ / ____
Miscellaneous	50 / 487	____ / ____	____ / ____	____ / ____

*BLOW MONEY   100 / 387   ____ / ____   ____ / ____   ____ / ____

RECREATION

*Entertainment	50 / 337	____ / ____	____ / ____	____ / ____
Vacation	25 / 312	____ / ____	____ / ____	____ / ____

DEBTS (Hopefully None)

Visa 1	100 / 212	____ / ____	____ / ____	____ / ____
Visa 2	____ / ____	____ / ____	____ / ____	____ / ____
MasterCard 1	75 / 137	____ / ____	____ / ____	____ / ____
MasterCard 2	____ / ____	____ / ____	____ / ____	____ / ____
American Express	50 / 87	____ / ____	____ / ____	____ / ____
Discover Card	____ / ____	____ / ____	____ / ____	____ / ____
Gas Card 1	____ / ____	____ / ____	____ / ____	____ / ____
Gas Card 2	____ / ____	____ / ____	____ / ____	____ / ____
Dept. Store Card 1	____ / ____	____ / ____	____ / ____	____ / ____
Dept. Store Card 2	____ / ____	____ / ____	____ / ____	____ / ____
Finance Co. 1	____ / ____	____ / ____	____ / ____	____ / ____
Finance Co. 2	____ / ____	____ / ____	____ / ____	____ / ____
Credit Line	____ / ____	____ / ____	____ / ____	____ / ____
Student Loan 1	87 / 0	____ / ____	12 / 0	____ / ____
Student Loan 2	____ / ____	____ / ____	____ / ____	____ / ____
Other _____	____ / ____	____ / ____	____ / ____	____ / ____
Other _____	____ / ____	____ / ____	____ / ____	____ / ____

Irregular Income Planning

Many people have an "irregular" income, which simply means that their compensation fluctuates from month to month. This is especially common for the self-employed, as well as commission-based salespeople. While this makes it more difficult to predict your income, you are still responsible for doing a monthly budget!

The "Monthly Cash Flow Plan" should remain a crucial part of your plan, as it lays out exactly how much money you need to bring home each month to survive and prosper. However, instead of doing the "Allocated Spending Plan," you will use this "Irregular Income Planning" sheet.

On this form, simply look at the individual items from your "Monthly Cash Flow Plan" sheet and prioritize them by importance. Ask yourself, "If I only have enough money to pay one thing, what would that be?" Put that at the top of your list. Then, ask yourself, "If I only have enough money to pay one more thing, what would that be?" That's number two. Keep this up all the way down the list.

With your list in place, you're ready to get paid. If you get a $1,500 paycheck, you will spend that $1,500 right down the list until it is gone, recording the cumulative amount spent in the "Cumulative Amount" column. At that point, you're finished spending, no matter what remains unpaid on the list. That's why the most important things are at the top of the list, right?

Be prepared to stand your ground. Things usually have a way of seeming important when they are only urgent. For example, a once-in-a-lifetime opportunity to see your favorite band perform live may seem important, but in reality, it is only urgent, meaning that it is time-sensitive. Urgency alone should not move an item to the top of this list!

ITEM	AMOUNT	CUMULATIVE AMOUNT
JC Penney	$150	$150
Sears	$250	$400
Visa	$500	$900
Vacation – part	$200	$1100
Christmas	$400	$1500

Breakdown of Savings

After you have fully funded your emergency fund, you can start to save for other items, such as furniture, car replacement, home maintenance, or a vacation. This sheet will remind you that every dollar in your savings account is already committed to something. For example, it's a bad idea to take money away from car repairs to pay for an impulse Hawaiian vacation, even if you pay cash for it. What would you do if the car broke down the week you got back home? However, it can be okay to reassign the dollars to another category, as long as you do it on purpose and it doesn't put you in a pinch in another category. Keep up with your breakdown of savings every month.

ITEM		BALANCE BY MONTH		
		October	November	December
Emergency Fund (1)	$1,000			
Emergency Fund (2)	3-6 months			
Retirement Fund				
College Fund				
Real Estate Taxes				
Homeowner's Insurance				
Repairs or Mn. Fee				
Replace Furniture				
Car Insurance				
Car Replacement		$600	$700	$800
Disability Insurance				
Health Insurance		$500	$500	$500
Doctor				
Dentist				
Optometrist				
Life Insurance				
School Tuition				
School Supplies				
Gifts (incl. Christmas)		$500	$650	$800
Vacation				
Other _____				
Other _____				
TOTAL		$1,600	$1,850	$2,100

Basic Student Budget

ITEM	MONTHLY TOTAL	ACCOUNT
GIVING	_____	_____
SAVING	_____	_____
HOUSING		
Rent	_____	_____
Rental Insurance	_____	_____
UTILITIES		
Cell Phone	_____	_____
Food	_____	_____
Electric	_____	_____
Cable	_____	_____
Internet	_____	_____
TRANSPORTATION		
Car Payment	_____	_____
Gas	_____	_____
Oil Change	_____	_____
Repairs & Tires	_____	_____
Car Insurance	_____	_____
CLOTHING	_____	_____
PERSONAL		
Health Insurance	_____	_____
Entertainment	_____	_____
OTHER MISC.	_____	_____
TOTAL MONTHLY NECESSITIES	_____	

Vocabulary

Active
ATM Card
Budget
Carbon Checks
Currency
Debit Card
Discipline
Envelope System
Hoarding
Impulse Purchase
Persistent
Pro-active
Procrastinate
Reconcile
Zero-based Budget

Matching

a. budget
b. irregular income form
c. monthly cash flow form
d. duplicate checks
e. reconcile
f. currency

___ 1. Form used to do a budget

___ 2. Form used by persons earning an inconsistent monthly income

___ 3. Process used to determine if the balance in your checking registry matches the balance reported on the bank statement

___ 4. Another name for cash flow plan

___ 5. Helps people who forget to record checks in their register after writing them

True or False

___ 6. You need to do a zero-based budget.

___ 7. You will pay interest on debit card purchases.

___ 8. A budget will be the same each and every month.

___ 9. You need to reconcile your bank statement within 72 hours of receiving it.

___ 10. People who don't earn a consistent salary monthly, do not have to do a budget.

Multiple Choice

11. Bounced checks are a sign of _____ living.
    a. normal
    b. crisis
    c. comfortable
    d. both a and b

12. A written budget should be done every
    a. month
    b. week
    c. 3 months
    d. 6 months

13. Your monthly budget should include
    a. fixed expenses
    b. variable expenses
    c. money to blow
    d. all of the above

14. What would account for a difference in balances in your checkbook registry and bank statement after reconciling the two?
    a. an error or omission
    b. outstanding checks that didn't clear
    c. deposits that did not post
    d. all of the above

15. Doing a budget does not:
    a. lead to an increase in arguments
    b. make your money go farther
    c. show if you are overspending in an area
    d. remove guilt and shame sometimes associated with purchases

Short Answer

16. Explain how to complete a zero based budget.

17. What are some reasons why the balance in your checkbook registry might not match the balance on your bank statement.

18. Why do you need a written budget even when you know you can afford your expenses?

19. How does a budget differ when you have an irregular income vs. a predictable income?

20. How can a budget help when you are working on Baby Step 2?

Case Studies

21. Paul just received his bank statement in the mail. The ending balance on the account showed that he had $385.22 available. However, last night on the way to the movies, Paul stopped at the ATM and withdrew $20. The ATM receipt showed a balance of only $174.38. What are some possible reasons for the difference in balances?

22. Kimberly works for a well known financial company as a sales representative. She earns a small base salary but receives commission off every product she sells. Kimberly has basic living expenses (rent, utilities, food, gas, car insurance etc.) in addition to a student loan. She wants to start adding to her Roth IRA and buy a new television and sound system for her house. She never knows what her monthly income will be due to the commissions. What advice can you give her to help her meet her goals?

23. Neal and Catherine recently graduated from college and are starting a family. Currently, they are just making ends meet with their $45,000 salary. They want to contribute the maximum amount (currently $2,000) to fully fund an Educational Savings Account when their baby is born. How much additional money will they need to budget every month and what are some things they can do to their budget to find the money?

BARGAIN SHOPPING  CH 8

What do other high school students know about bargain shopping?

We asked high school students to tell us about the best deal they've ever negotiated:

> " I negotiated the price of my vehicle by pulling cash out of my pocket. **I got it for $350 less than the asking price.** "
>
> Senior, Oklahoma

"When I was in New York City, I went to Chinatown and got $100 perfume for $30. I told the guy that was all the money I had."

Junior, New Mexico

"I went to the pawn shop to buy a CD player for my car and the owner wanted $80. I told him I would go somewhere else to get it cheaper, and then he sold it to me for $60."

Junior, Oklahoma

"I found a brand new $350 fish tank at a yard sale for just $15."

Sophomore, Florida

"I waited until July 5th to buy fireworks. The salesman had to get rid of his supplies so I got hundreds of bottle rockets for $25."

Senior, Georgia

LEARNING OUTCOMES

Explain why you should be honest when negotiating.

Analyze and use the three keys to getting bargains.

Describe the seven basic rules of negotiating.

List places to find a great deal.

KEY TERMS

Auction
Consignment Shop
Estate Sale
Foreclosures
Integrity
Markup
Negotiating
Patience
Walk Away Power
Win-Win

119

BEFORE YOU BEGIN

What do you know about bargain shopping?

Answer the following questions before you watch the lesson. Discuss your answers as a class.

Agree	Disagree		
☐	☐	1.	Most of the items at a pawn shop are stolen.
☐	☐	2.	Learning to be quiet is actually a powerful tool in negotiation.
☐	☐	3.	A seller who senses that you are attached to an item will be less likely to negotiate a deal.
☐	☐	4.	In certain circumstances, it is OK to stretch the truth to get a bargain.
☐	☐	5.	Excluding the United States, most countries use negotiating as a way of life.

In what stores do you shop most frequently?

....

....

Explain the best deal you ever negotiated.

....

....

List places that you are likely to find great deals.

....

....

Buying Only Big, Big Bargains

It is proper to get a great deal if you:

1. Have in no way _____ the truth.

2. Have not set out to _____ the other party.

3. Have created a _____ - _____ deal.

The First Key

The first key to opening the door to huge bargains is learning to _____ everything.

Win-win deals really work, so don't be _____ to _____ for the deal.

Seven Basic Rules of Negotiating

1. Always tell the absolute _____. ◀ END OF VIDEO PART 1

2. Use the power of _____.

   ▸ Cash is _____.

   ▸ Cash is _____.

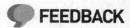

💬 **FEEDBACK**

People in other cultures routinely use negotiation when buying and selling goods. Do you have any experience negotiating overseas?

"I bartered in Mexico and paid $3 for a ring that started at $10."

Senior, Florida

"It's so fun to negotiate in Germany and see how low you can get the seller to go on his price."

Junior, New Mexico

"In Mexico, I got a $50 chain for $15."

Junior, Michigan

"Once I negotiated in Mexico and paid half the price listed."

Senior, Missouri

"You can bargain at the straw market in the Bahamas. I talked the sales rep at a brand name purse shop down from $150 to $40."

Senior, Georgia

💲 MONEY FACTS

Teens spent **$179 billion** in 2006, or **$102 per week** each.

Teenage Research Unlimited

57% of teens say they know how to shop for the best deal when making a purchase.

Charles Schwab Survey

27% of teens report using PayPal or another account designed for online transactions.

Charles Schwab Survey

Teen girls spend more in a typical week than teen boys.

Charles Schwab Survey

▶ Cash has _____.

END OF VIDEO PART 2

3. Understand and use " _____ _____ power."

4. _____ _____.

5. "That's not _____ _____."

6. _____ guy, _____ guy. END OF VIDEO PART 3

7. The "If I _____ _____ technique."

If you are patient, willing to negotiate, and educated about what items are on sale during certain seasons, you'll be saving big before you know it!

The Second Key

The second key to opening the door to huge bargains is that you must have _____.

Don't get _____ to a purchase.

The Third Key

The third key to opening the door to huge bargains is that you must know _____ to _____ deals.

_____ something of value, goods or just your _____.

"I have used your tips for negotiating and they really work. But how can I get the most money for items I sell? I don't want to get ripped off and I'm not sure how to go about this wisely. Do you have any tips?"

DAVE'S ANSWER: That's a good question and you are right, you don't want to get ripped off when you sell things. First, don't play all your cards face up. The buyer will see that you really need the money. Make it clear that you have walk away power as a seller. If you can't get the price you want, just walk away from the deal. In the case of antiques or collectible items, get them appraised and sell them slightly below that price. Showing the buyer that you are selling for less than the appraisal will make them feel like they are getting a deal. At the same time, you'll know it was a win-win deal because you were armed with information. Try these things, and like everything else, you will get better with practice.

"I've heard you teach people to always watch for deals and ask for bargains on whatever they want to buy. Have you ever totaled up how much money you've saved in a single year by bargaining?"

DAVE'S ANSWER: No, I haven't. That might be a fun experiment to try some time. I do know that one year my wife added up all of the money she saved by using coupons at the grocery store and it came to over $600 that year—just by using coupons to buy things we were going to buy anyway. Seeing those savings really made an impact on how we feel about bargain hunting and using coupons to save money.

Places to Find Great Deals

1. _____

                                             ◄ END OF VIDEO PART 4

2. _____ Sales

3. _____ _____

4. Couponing

💲 MONEY FACTS

16 to 18 percent of Americans shop at thrift stores each year.

America's Research Group

There are more than **2,000** not-for-profit stores of Goodwill Industries and these stores recently had **$1.8 billion** in retail sales.

National Association of Resale and Thrift Shops

5. _____ _____

6. Repo Lot

7. _____ _____

8. Refunding

9. _____

10. _____ Shops

11. _____ _____

12. _____ Ads

13. _____ _____

14. Conventions

END OF VIDEO PART 5

🏵 REAL LIFE

You may not be the bargain-buying, negotiating type, but if you're going to make the most of your money, you'll have to start looking for ways to save money by shopping for big, big bargains.

Here are some tips to help stretch your hard earned money.

1. **Keep your eye on the calendar.** If you buy your winter clothes in the summer and your summer clothes in the winter, you can literally save hundreds. Even if you buy a car or house during the off seasons, you can save big. That whole supply-and-demand thing really is true!

2. **Get outdated technology.** Be willing to buy last year's models of TVs, DVDs, computers and digital cameras and you can save tons. Chances are the bells and whistles added to the latest versions aren't worth the extra money!

3. **Comparison shop.** You may always shop at one particular store, but venture out to find big bargains at stores you may have never visited before. Discount stores and second-hand shops are fantastic places to find deals and save big-time! You can even hop online to find sites that compare products and stores to help you find the best value.

4. **Make a deal.** Don't be afraid to negotiate for a lower price. If you're shopping with cash, your chances of making a sweet deal are a lot better.

5. **Get to know eBay.** Buying stuff at online auction sites is another way to get nice, slightly used items. Just make sure you buy from reputable sellers with a high positive feedback ranking.

A Recipe for Becoming a Millionaire

- $1000 in the bank
- 1 cup of silence
- 4 tablespoons of negotiation
- 3 baby steps (sliced)
- Half a cup of income
- A pinch of devotion

- 2 handfuls of attitude
- A dash of savings (extra if you need it)
- 40 ounces of no debt (most important ingredient)
- 5 handfuls of cash (grade A)

Set oven to 450 degrees. In a large bowl start with $1,000 in the bank. Add 3 baby steps (sliced). Stir until thick. Next put in a pinch of devotion (some people will definitely need this). Once this has settled for a few minutes, add a dash of savings, extra if you need it. This will loosen it up. Finally stir in a half of a cup of income. Stir, and set aside.

Grab a medium bowl and put in 5 handfuls of cash (grade A). Mix in 1 cup of silence (a key ingredient, hint: goes well with negotiation). Next, add 4 tablespoons of negotiation and slowly pour in 40 ounces of no debt (the recipe will not work without this). Finally, add the last ingredient, 2 handfuls of attitude (also goes well with negotiation).

Grab the other ingredients you set aside and carefully spread on top of the mixture. Slide this into the oven and cook until golden brown. Let cool.

Congratulations, you now know the recipe for becoming a millionaire. Warning: all ingredients have to be used and accounted for, or you will have to start over.

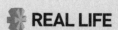 **REAL LIFE**

Want to become a millionaire? Try this recipe by **Caitlin Parker**, an Alabama high school student.

Recap and Review

Don't be afraid to ask for the deal.

Use cash as it has power.

Don't forget walk away power.

Silence can make a huge difference in your favor when negotiating.

Remember these words "THAT'S NOT GOOD ENOUGH."

 **WISE GUYS**

"Remember, what you possess in the world will be found at the day of your death to belong to someone else, but what you are will be yours forever."

Henry Van Dyke

Vocabulary

Auction
Consignment Shop
Estate Sale
Foreclosures
Integrity
Mark-Up
Negotiating
Patience
Walk Away Power
Win-Win

Matching

a. auctions
b. estate sale
c. integrity
d. rebating
e. walk-away power
f. win-win
g. patience

____ 1. The opposite of showing that you are hooked on a purchase

____ 2. Always telling the absolute truth

____ 3. Waiting without becoming upset

____ 4. Both parties benefit

____ 5. Sending in proof of purchase, receiving cash back

____ 6. Type of sale used to dispose of a majority of items owned by a person

True or False

____ 7. Knowing how to talk to a salesman is one of the most powerful and pressure oriented things in negotiation.

____ 8. When negotiating, you must use integrity and avoid misrepresenting the truth.

____ 9. You can get great deals if you find a convention that is just setting up.

____ 10. Couponing is when you send in proof of purchase to get cash back.

____ 11. Gathering information on what the other person's needs, wants, and fears is only a small part of successful negotiation.

Fill in the Blank

12. _____ guy, _____ guy

13. _____-up

14. _____ -away power

15. That's _____ _____ enough

Short Answer

16. What are some of the reasons most people don't negotiate?

17. What are some things that you have recently negotiated (may not all have to do with purchases)?

18. Evaluate the role research has to do with successful bargain shopping. List as many as you can.

19. Explain how walk away power and silence are powerful tools of negotiation.

20. If you had to place the three keys of successful negotiating in order of importance, which would you put first and why?

Case Studies

21. Sean is wanting to buy a friend's car but does not have the $3,000 that is being asked. He has $2,500 and is considering borrowing the extra $500 from his sister. Sean is considering telling his friend that he needs the extra $500 for a deposit at the college he will attend next year. Sean knows his parents will be paying for this expense but feels this might be a good negotiating technique to save some money. What should he do?

22. Ethan and Julia are newly married, on a tight budget and expecting a baby. At a yard sale, they see a nice baby bed within their budget but wonder if using someone else's baby bed is in bad taste. They are also afraid that their friends will think they are cheap if they start buying used things for the baby? Ethan and Julia are considering a retail store to find something new. What should they do?

23. Terry is interested in biking because his friends ride a lot. He doesn't want to spend a lot of money on his first good bike because he is not sure how much he will like riding. Terry figures he can always upgrade if he enjoys the sport. He went to the bike shop and found their prices to be expensive for a beginner. Does he have to pay retail to get a good bike? Explain.

RELATING WITH MONEY  CH 9

What do other high school students know about relating with money?

We asked high school students if they've ever witnessed money affecting a relationship close to them:

> " **Money is always a strain at my house. At least every other day, my parents fight about money.** "
>
> Junior, Michigan

"When my parents fight, it is usually concerning a purchase that didn't get recorded in the checkbook."

Senior, Wyoming

"Money was the cause of my parents' divorce when I was five years old."

Senior, Oklahoma

"My parents fought all the time about money and are now divorcing."

Senior, Alabama

"My parents argue about what they spend money on and what bills need to be paid first."

Sophomore, Florida

LEARNING OUTCOMES

Explain the difference between a commission and an allowance.

Describe the general differences that exist between men and women as they relate to money.

Identify the characteristics of a nerd and a free spirit and explain how they approach the budget in different ways.

Evaluate the importance of doing a budget together when married.

KEY TERMS

Accountability
Allowance
Commission
Fiscal
Free Spirit
Nerd
Work Ethic

BEFORE YOU BEGIN

What do you know about relating with money?

Before you watch the Relating with Money lesson, take the following survey to see if you have more free spirit or nerd tendencies. Check the characteristics that best describe you.

FREE SPIRITS tend to be:	NERDS tend to be:
☐ Creative	☐ Number-oriented (enjoy working with numbers)
☐ Spontaneous	☐ Rule followers
☐ Less organized and not concerned about rules	☐ Organized
☐ Late for meetings, dates, appointments—most everything	☐ On time for everything
☐ Easy going	☐ Slow and steady when making decisions

What are your initial thoughts about relating with money?

....

....

....

....

....

....

....

....

What do you want to learn about relating with money?

....

....

....

....

....

....

....

....

Men, Women and Money (over-generalizing)

The flow of money in a family represents the _____ _____ under which that family operates.

Emergency Fund Savings

Men: "It's boring and not _____ enough."

Women: "It's the most _____ key to our financial plan."

Shopping

Men get good deals by _____. They want to win.

Women get good deals by _____. They enjoy the process.

> END OF VIDEO PART 1

Financial Problems

Men lose _____ - _____ because money usually represents a _____ to them.

Women face _____ or even _____ because, with women, money usually represents _____.

Information not otherwise sourced in this section is largely based off of Dave Ramsey's personal experience in counseling families for over 20 years, as well as his experience in talking with more than 5,000 radio listeners and television viewers every year.

! STUPID TAX

"I bought a monkey and my mom grounded me."

Junior, Alabama

"When I got my first paycheck, I spent every dollar of it the same day at the mall."

Senior, Tennessee

"It took me a couple of months, but I finally had over $600 saved up. Then, I took this girl I really liked to a Valentine's Day dance and spent about $300. Now I really regret doing that."

Senior, Utah

Marriage and Money

The number one cause of divorce in America is

_____ _____.

When you agree on your value system, you will reach a

_____ in your marriage that you can experience no

other way.

Who does the Financial Decision-Making?

_____ of you!

The partner with the natural _____ can prepare

the _____, but the decision-making must be

done by both of you. **END OF VIDEO PART 2**

The _____ likes doing the budget because it gives

them control, and they feel like they are taking care of

loved ones.

The _____ _____ feels controlled, not cared for, and

can appear irresponsible to the nerd. **END OF VIDEO PART 3**

Singles and Money

_____ _____ and fatigue can lead to

poor money management.

REAL LIFE

Marriage counselor Gary Smalley identifies five behavioral differences concerning men and women in his book, *Making Love Last Forever.*

Men love to share facts, **women** love to express feelings.

Men connect by doing things, **women** connect by talking.

Men tend to compete, **women** tend to cooperate.

Men tend to be controlling, **women** tend to remain agreeable.

Men tend to be independent, **women** tend to be interdependent.

"My boyfriend's credit is in bad shape and we're thinking about getting married someday. Will his bad credit rating affect mine? My credit is in good shape right now."

DAVE'S ANSWER: Marrying someone with a bad credit rating will not affect your score. In other words, the black marks on his credit rating don't jump across the aisle onto your report as soon as he slips the ring on your finger.

After you're married, your husband will be listed as "spouse" on your report. Then, if they pull your report for any reason, they'll see that half of your "team" has had some problems in the past. When the two of you decide to buy a home, it may be difficult if there are still problems with his credit report.

But the big issue here is that you seem to have differing views on money management. Make sure you go through premarital counseling together, and begin the process of working together to make monthly budgets. If you get married, money is going to be a big part of your lives for a long time. Agreeing on your goals now will set the foundation for your dreams.

Beware of _____ buying, which can be brought on by _____ or even by the "I owe it to _____" syndrome.

A written plan gives the single person _____, self-accountability and _____.

Prevention

Develop an _____ relationship.

This is someone with whom to discuss major _____.

This is someone with whom to discuss your _____.

Accountability friends must love you enough to be brutally honest and promise to do so for your own good.

WISE GUYS

"Personal relationships are the fertile soil from which all advancement, all success, all achievement in real life grows."

Ben Stein

"Tell me, and I'll forget. Show me, and I may not remember. Involve me, and I'll understand."

Native American Saying

Kids and Money

Teaching kids how to handle money is not the _____ responsibility. It is the parents' responsibility.

Parents should pay _____, not allowance; we have enough people in our society who expect to be made allowance for.

Words are _____.

If you _____, you get paid; if you do not _____, you do not get paid.

Teach by _____.

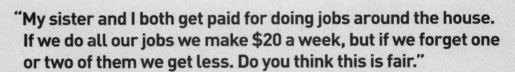

"My sister and I both get paid for doing jobs around the house. If we do all our jobs we make $20 a week, but if we forget one or two of them we get less. Do you think this is fair."

DAVE'S ANSWER: Yes, I think that's very fair. I love the fact that your parents have put you on a commission system instead of just handing you money.

In the real world, if you don't work you don't eat. You also won't have money to do other things like go to the movies or buy clothes. Learning the value of hard work and doing a job well is a very important lesson all kids should learn, and all parents should teach this to their children.

Think about how you feel on the weeks when you do all your jobs compared to the times you haven't. Work is rewarding financially. But the rewards won't be as great if you don't get the job done or do your work well!

Parents should show kids how to live _____ free, how insurance works, how an IRA works, etc.

Be Age-Appropriate

If the children are young, use a clear _____ to save. Visual reinforcement is powerful. `END OF VIDEO PART 4`

Use three envelopes for ages 5-12: _____, _____ and _____.

Somewhere around 13-15 years old, open a _____ _____ for the child and teach him/her how to run it by monthly reviews. `END OF VIDEO PART 5`

Recap and Review

How you handle money will affect all of your relationships.

Make sure you understand how you relate to money. Are you a nerd or a free spirit?

Men and women are different when it comes to money.

Understanding how you personally relate to money will lead to better communication and relationships.

$ MONEY FACTS

52% of teens say they simply ask for money from their parents or guardians when they want or need something.

Fewer than **41%** of teens get money from an allowance whether tied to chores or not.

Charles Schwab Survey

Vocabulary

Accountability
Allowance
Commission
Fiscal
Free Spirit
Nerd
Self-Esteem
Value System
Work Ethic

Matching

a. free spirit
b. nerd
c. value system
d. allowance
e. commission
f. accountability

____ 1. The one who likes to deal with numbers and make a budget

____ 2. Getting paid based on the work you complete

____ 3. The one who goes with the flow

____ 4. Taking responsibility and assisting with wise decisions

____ 5. What is important to you

True or False

____ 6. The number one cause of divorce in the U.S. is money fights.

____ 7. You need to get a shopping partner to discuss major purchases with.

____ 8. Men and women are quite similar in how they relate to money.

____ 9. Nerds are always the savers and free spirits are always the spenders.

____ 10. Personal finance is 80% behavior and only 20% head-knowledge.

Multiple Choice

11. For _____ ,the emergency fund is the most important key to financial security.
    a. women
    b. men
    c. both
    d. Dave Ramsey

12. How do men and women relate differently to shopping?
    a. Men want to find a good deal by hunting; women want to find a good deal by negotiating.
    b. Women want to find a good deal by hunting; men want to find a good deal by negotiating.
    c. Women enjoy the process of looking; men want to win by getting the deal.
    d. all of the above
    e. both b and c

13. A budget committee meeting should last:
    a. 45 minutes
    b. as long as it takes
    c. 10-20 minutes
    d. no more than an hour

14. Children who save money to buy their own car are:
    a. less likely to appreciate the car because they will have to settle for a cheaper car
    b. more likely to appreciate and take care of a car they saved for
    c. more likely to learn fiscal responsibility
    d. both b and c

15. Which one is not a rule for a budget committee meeting?
    a. free spirits must give input
    b. the meeting should last no longer than 20 minutes
    c. nerds must not let the free spirits change anything on their budget
    d. all of the above are ground rules for a budget meeting

Short Answer

16. Explain the advantages and disadvantages that singles have when it comes to finances.

17. How does getting an allowance differ from earning a commission?

18. What are some things you can do to teach young children about money?

19. Are you a free spirit or a nerd? Explain the characteristics you have.

20. Compare how men and women differ when it comes to an emergency fund.

Case Studies

21. David and Melissa want to teach their 18-year-old son, Jim, how to handle money responsibly. Jim has no interest in going to college but wants to work so he can make money to hang out with his friends. Jim's parents bought him a car for his birthday and he only has to pay for gas because his parents pay his insurance. David and Melissa are afraid that Jim is not going to graduate high school because his grades are slipping, but Jim is not worried. What advice would Dave give to David and Melissa?

22. Mark just graduated from college and landed a sales job with a starting salary of $45,000 per year. He has one student loan on which he is making double payments and a fully-funded emergency fund. Mark is about to ask his girlfriend, Erin, to marry him. Erin has a car payment and uses a credit card for purchases, although she does pay the balance in full each month. She also has a pretty good job but no savings. Mark wants to make sure that they are on the same page financially when they get married. What does he need to do to make sure that happens?

23. Julie is having a hard time convincing her husband, Erik, to do a budget. His income is $35,000, but he also works a part-time job so he has extra spending money. They have credit card debt and some minor medical bills. Julie wants to get out of debt but Erik thinks that everything is fine. Julie calls Dave on the air to discuss her situation. What does Dave tell her?

INSURANCE/RISK MANAGEMENT
and INCOME/CAREERS

CAREER CHOICES and TAXES

What do other high school students know about taxes?

We asked high school students to tell us what they know about taxes and if they've ever had to pay any:

" I pay them, **but I don't know what they are.**

Junior, Wyoming "

"They are taken out of my check for government spending, Social Security and Medicare."

Senior, Texas

"The government takes a percentage of your earnings from each check."

Junior, Florida

"I know that you have to pay taxes on just about everything that you buy."

Senior, Missouri

"I know that you have to pay income taxes, but if you file a return, you'll get money back."

Junior, Oklahoma

LEARNING OUTCOMES

Identify your personal strengths and weaknesses.

Evaluate the role of a cover letter, résumé and interview.

Explain the various types of taxes withheld from your paycheck.

KEY TERMS

Career
Cover Letter
Deduction
FICA
Income Tax
Interview
Payroll Deduction
Résumé

BEFORE YOU BEGIN

What do you know about choosing a career?

The majority of the next lesson is about choosing a career that blends your strengths, interests, abilities and personality traits. Whether you are going to college or straight into the workforce, you will need to be able to answer some basic questions about yourself. The answers to these questions will help to not only guide you in your career path, but to prepare you for interviews as well. Take some time to answer these questions:

1. What are your strengths?

2. What are your weaknesses?

3. What are your career goals?

4. How would you describe yourself?

5. Describe your ability to work as part of a team.

6. Why should we hire you (or accept you into this program)?

Change Happens

The average job is now only _____ years in length.

This means that the average worker could have as many as _____ different jobs in his or her working lifetime.

Small business is changing the way we think about work. _____ of the companies in America have fewer than 100 employees.

Discover Your Strengths and Weaknesses

How can you know _____ you ought to be and _____ you ought to be doing if you don't know _____ you are?

Speaker and author Marcus Buckingham has identified some common myths that often rob people of having fulfillment and enjoyment in their careers.

▶ MYTH: As you grow, you _____.

▶ TRUTH: You do not _____ your personality.

FEEDBACK

We asked high school students what they wanted to do when they got out of school and how much money they thought they would make. The most frequent answer was "go to college and make a lot of money." Here are some of the more interesting choices:

Pro basketball player
Translator
Orthopedic surgeon
FBI agent
Marine biologist
Physical therapist
Traveling nurse
Photojournalist
Anesthesiologist
Advertising/Marketing
Pro baseball player
Navy SEAL
Obstetrician
Plumber
Movie producer
Army Ranger
Explosives expert
Pro tennis player
Sports agent

$ MONEY FACTS

Less than **39%** of people under the age of 25 are satisfied with their jobs.
MSNBC

4 out of 5
Americans do not have their dream job.
careerbuilder.com

Only **14%** of teens know how income taxes work.
Charles Schwab Survey

69% of teens report that the amount of money they can make will influence the career they choose.
Charles Schwab Survey

73% of teens believe they'll be earning plenty of money when they're out on their own.
Charles Schwab Survey

Based on the career that most interests them, teens believe they'll be earning an average annual salary of **$145,500** (boys expect to earn $173,000 vs. girls $114,200).
Charles Schwab Survey

The median annual household income is **$48,201.**
U.S. Census Bureau

▶ MYTH: You will learn and grow the most in the areas in which you are _____.

▶ TRUTH: You grow in your _____. You will grow the most in the areas that you already know and love the most. **END OF VIDEO PART 1**

Identify Your Motivation and Passion

Career coach Dan Miller reminds us that _____ is ultimately never enough compensation for doing a job.

Find something that blends your skills, _____, personality traits, _____, dreams and _____.

Understanding Your Unique Personality

The _____ profile is a simple test that will yield tremendous insight into how you process decisions and what your natural tendencies may be.

▶ The D (_____) person is a hard-charging driver that is task-oriented and first looks to _____.

▶ The I (_____) person is people-oriented, fun, outgoing and generally concerned about people-pleasing, so they first look to _____.

▶ The S (_____) person is amiable, loyal, does not like conflict, and is concerned about _____.

▶ The C (_____) person is analytical, loves detail, factual, can seem rigid, and loves _____.

◀ END OF VIDEO PART 2

MORE INFO

In American culture, too many people spend a lifetime chasing wealth in a career that they hate. Or, they work an excessive number of hours every week. "Do not wear yourself out to get rich. Have the wisdom to show restraint." (Proverbs 23:4-5) Do something you love and that is fun for you! If you make a lot of money, great! But if you don't, at least you will have spent a lifetime doing something that was rewarding. Money should never become your primary motivation.

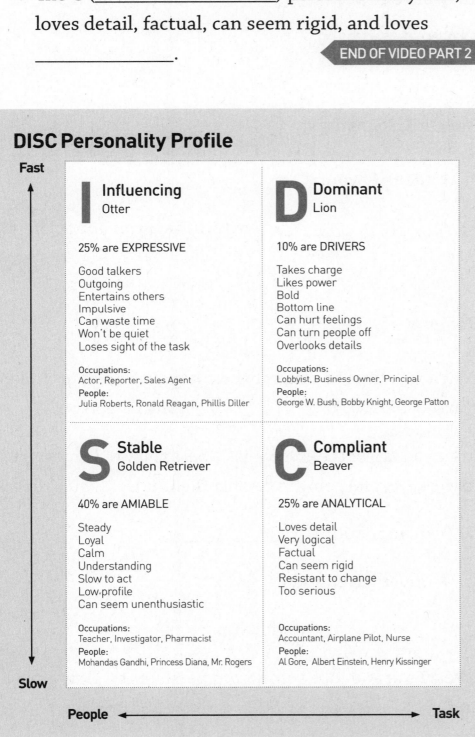

DISC Personality Profile

Fast

I Influencing
Otter

25% are EXPRESSIVE

Good talkers
Outgoing
Entertains others
Impulsive
Can waste time
Won't be quiet
Loses sight of the task

Occupations:
Actor, Reporter, Sales Agent
People:
Julia Roberts, Ronald Reagan, Phillis Diller

D Dominant
Lion

10% are DRIVERS

Takes charge
Likes power
Bold
Bottom line
Can hurt feelings
Can turn people off
Overlooks details

Occupations:
Lobbyist, Business Owner, Principal
People:
George W. Bush, Bobby Knight, George Patton

S Stable
Golden Retriever

40% are AMIABLE

Steady
Loyal
Calm
Understanding
Slow to act
Low-profile
Can seem unenthusiastic

Occupations:
Teacher, Investigator, Pharmacist
People:
Mohandas Gandhi, Princess Diana, Mr. Rogers

C Compliant
Beaver

25% are ANALYTICAL

Loves detail
Very logical
Factual
Can seem rigid
Resistant to change
Too serious

Occupations:
Accountant, Airplane Pilot, Nurse
People:
Al Gore, Albert Einstein, Henry Kissinger

Slow

People ◀——————▶ Task

WISE GUYS

"To find out what one is fitted to do, and to secure an opportunity to do it, is the key to happiness."

John Dewey

"Life is never made unbearable by circumstances but only by lack of meaning and purpose."

Viktor Frankl

"Know thyself, and to thine own self be true."

Shakespeare

"The unexamined life is not worth living."

Socrates

"Until you make peace with who you are, you will never be content with what you have."

Doris Mortman

"The secret of success is focus of purpose."

Thomas Edison

"Think beyond your lifetime if you want to accomplish something truly worthwhile."

Walt Disney

Job Hunting

Companies do not start out looking for _____. They have a specific _____ and they need someone to meet it.

Develop a Strategy:

▶ Identify your _____.

▶ _____ everything you can about them.

Résumés

When it is time to contact the company, think of it like starting a new _____ with a person.

After you target the companies where you would most like to work, you are going to contact them at least three times.

▶ Introduction _____.

▶ Cover letter and Résumé.

▶ _____ follow-up.

Interviews and jobs come from persistent follow-up and _____.

Sample Résumé

John Q. Public

402111 Little Drive
Lamponia, TN 13579
johnp@example.com
555-123-4567

OBJECTIVE
To obtain a position working as a camp counselor.

EDUCATION

Completed three years of college prep coursework at Washington High School.
Projected graduation date: May 2009 GPA: 3.0

WORK EXPERIENCE

Junior Reserve Officer Training Corps, Lamponia High School (2007-present)
   ➢ Rank: Sergeant First Class
Jeffrey's Grille, Lamponia (2006-present)
   ➢ Salad prep and fry cook
   ➢ Bus boy and dishwasher

VOLUNTEER POSITIONS

Crew Leader, YMCA Summer Camp (2004-2008)
   ➢ Guided children in various activities
   ➢ Assisted children with creative projects
Coaching Assistant, Lamponia Middle School Wrestling Program (2006-2008)
   ➢ Coached athletes in the sport of wrestling
   ➢ Educated athletes about wrestling
   ➢ Prepared facilities for tournaments
Coaching Assistant, Thompson County Wrestling Club (2006-2008)
Program Volunteer, Lamponia Community Church, Homeless Ministry (2005-2008)
   ➢ Enlisted homeless men in games, activities, and conversation

EXTRACURRICULAR ACTIVITIES

Wrestling Team, Lamponia Middle School
Junior Varsity Wrestling Team, Lamponia High School, 2005-present
   ➢ Iron Man Award
Wrestling Clubs
   ➢ Thompson County Wrestling Club
   ➢ Hopeville Jr. Wrestling Club
   ➢ Lamponia Wrestling Club

MONEY FACTS

These figures show what the average person earns in relation to their level of education. It pays to stay in school. These figures are averages, and while education increases the probability of earning more, it is not a guarantee

$24,721
High School Dropout

$33,419
High School Diploma

$38,284
Some College

$41,475
Associate's Degree

$58,866
Bachelor's Degree

$70,813
Master's Degree

U.S. Census Bureau

MORE INFO

The Internal Revenue Service (IRS) is the federal government agency responsible for tax collection and tax law enforcement. It was created during the Civil War in 1862 to enact a national income tax to pay for war expenses.

Interviews

Present yourself well. You are the _____, so make it the best one available.

Be on _____, address everyone by _____, offer a firm, confident _____, and maintain _____ contact at all times.

Designate a time to _____ _____ after the interview... and DO IT!

END OF VIDEO PART 3

Overtime and Extra Jobs

Raising your income _____ - term is a career track issue. Raising it _____ -term means the dreaded part-time job.

How do you get started with an extra job?

▶ Be willing to _____ to win.

▶ Have a detailed _____ so you can see the finish line. This gives you hope!

▶ Choose the _____ or start a _____ - _____ business.

"What kind of things can you put on a part-time job application that will make you stand out from everyone else?"

DAVE'S ANSWER: Experience is a great thing to have when you're looking for a job. Every employer wants to know that a potential employee can do the job.

But even if it's your first "real" job you probably have experience you didn't think about. Baby-sitting is great experience. It's even better if the parents will give you a good recommendation. If parents feel comfortable with you caring for their child, surely a fast food manager can trust you to flip a few burgers.

If you're in band, hold a seat on the student council, or even play sports, these things can catch a manager's eye. They all show that you're willing to work, commit to something, and take on responsibility.

"How should I dress for a part-time job interview?"

DAVE'S ANSWER: Whether a job is part-time or full-time, you should dress in a manner that's appropriate. This doesn't always mean a suit and tie, but it sure doesn't mean jeans and a concert t-shirt, either.

As much as anything, the way you dress for an interview says something about your level of maturity. Some managers even take it as an indication of respect—or lack thereof—and how much you really want the job.

I'd say a pair of khaki pants and a nice polo shirt would be appropriate for a guy, and a shirt with nice slacks for a girl. It wouldn't hurt to go one step further and dress up even nicer.

Think of it this way. If you were trying to get a potential girlfriend or boyfriend's attention, you'd fix yourself up nice, right? Well, in a job interview you're trying to get the owner's attention and win that job!

▶ Don't _____ _____!

Beware! Do not allow your work to be the source of all your satisfaction and self-_____.   `END OF VIDEO PART 4`

"What are some good starting jobs?"

DAVE'S ANSWER: There are two ways to look at your teen working career. One is you can do it simply for money. It might not be a job that will carry you where you want to go the rest of your life, but you would learn to work and you would be able to earn some money to meet some of your goals—buying a car or paying your insurance, for instance.

That could be a job like cutting grass. That's what I did as a teen—cut grass, did home repairs like painting, and all sorts of other manual labor. I don't do that today. It didn't really prepare me for today, except it taught me to estimate a job, complete a job, and to follow through with my promises. I did make really, really good money doing it, as opposed to my friends who were doing other jobs.

The other kind of job you can take is one that doesn't really pay you very much but that gives you a chance to participate in a career field in which you may end up working long term. You probably won't be doing anything except making copies and getting people coffee, but you'll get to learn the business by watching all of the insiders. You probably won't be paid anything, or maybe just a small amount, but the real value is the experience and education that will help you make career decisions later.

Recap and Review

Discover your strengths and weaknesses and identify what motivates you. This will help you decide your career path.

Money doesn't buy happiness. Do something you love and that blends your talents, skills and abilities.

Remember the importance of making a good first impression at the interview. This is the most important part of securing a job.

Taxes are part of everyday life and you should understand all of your payroll taxes.

Taxes, Deductions and Witholdings

Benjamin Franklin said, "Only two things in life are certain: death and taxes." Taxes are important to understand and you need to know about deductions and withholdings. The government relies on the revenue taxes create to meet their expenses and pay for services such as roads, education and social services. While the specifics differ from state to state, the government taxes three economic bases to pay for its programs: income, consumption and wealth. Like it or not, taxes are a part of everyday life.

Taxes on Income

April 15 is the deadline to file tax returns. Even young people just starting to work a few hours a week are required to file tax returns. According to the IRS, young people have to file taxes under certain conditions. Go to irs.gov for more information.

On your pay stub, you will notice three taxes taken out or deducted from your paycheck. These are commonly referred to as withholdings. When you get hired by a company, you will fill out a federal tax form called a W-4. The information on this form is the basis for determining how much income tax should be withheld from your paycheck. Payroll taxes, as these are commonly known, are a tax on income. Hence, you file an income tax return with the government every year you earn income. The three taxes are:

- Federal income tax, which is used to support government programs. This is where the federal government gets much of their money. You work. They spend.
- State income tax, which is used to support state services (if you work in a state without a state income tax, you will not have this withholding)
- FICA, which stands for Federal Insurance Contribution Act and pays for benefits that workers and families receive for either Social Security or Medicare. Social Security pays for benefits under the old-age survivors and disability insurance part of the act. Medicare pays for benefits under the hospital insurance part of the act.

Taxes on Consumption

The primary taxes on consumption are sales and excise tax.

- Sales tax is used by states as a source of their income and each state sets its own tax rate. Taxes on items such as cars, clothing and movie tickets are sales tax.
- Excise tax is levied on certain goods produced within a country and is sometimes referred to as luxury tax. This is used by both the state and federal government. Taxes on items such as gasoline, beer, liquor, cigarettes and airplane tickets are excise taxes.

Taxes on Wealth and Property

The primary taxes are wealth and property tax.

- Property tax is the main source of revenue for local governments. Taxes on land, private homes and business property are property taxes.
- Some states tax certain types of personal property. This might include cars, boats and recreational vehicles.
- Taxes on wealth include inheritance, estate and gift taxes.

Vocabulary

Career
Contact Letter
Cover Letter
Deduction
DISC Personality Profile
Excise Tax
FICA
Income Tax
Medicare
Motivation
Payroll Deduction
Sales Tax
Résumé
Stable
Vocation
W-4
Withholding

Matching

a. résumé
b. introductory letter
c. interview
d. gross pay
e. withholdings
f. cover letter
g. FICA
h. federal
i. net pay

___ 1. Taxes deducted from your paycheck

___ 2. Social Security and Medicare

___ 3. Your actual take home pay

___ 4. Your total wages from working

___ 5. Lists your skills, employment history and education

___ 6. Tax used for government programs

___ 7. A letter that addresses specific qualifications you have for a particular job

___ 8. Most important aspect of securing a job

___ 9. A letter to a prospective employer that you will be contacting them

True or False

___ 10. Most companies in the United States have over 100 employees.

___ 11. The average job in America lasts about five years.

___ 12. Classified ads account for a majority of available jobs.

___ 13. An important aspect of choosing a career path is looking at your interest.

___ 14. Getting a college degree does not ensure that you will be happy with your job.

___ 15. The rate of change is blinding so you must engage in the process of continual learning.

___ 16. FICA taxes fund both Social Security and Medicare.

___ 17. If you are under 17 years of age, you are not required to file a tax return.

____ 18. The primary source of revenue for local governments is property tax.

____ 19. The résumé is the most important aspect of securing a job.

Multiple Choice

20. Which of the following would not help you make a good first impression?
    a. multiple body piercings
    b. firm hand shake
    c. good eye contact
    d. arriving 10 minutes early

21. Résumés get you:
    a. careers
    b. contacts
    c. interviews
    d. all of the above

22. The key to finding work you love is to blend your:
    a. parent's interests
    b. personality traits
    c. skills
    d. both b and c

23. Which is not part of the personality profile?
    a. influencing
    b. dominant
    c. stable
    d. confident

24. What could you put on your résumé if you didn't have a lot of work experience?
    a. clubs and activities
    b. sports and accomplishments
    c. favorite band
    d. both a and b

25. Most hiring decisions are made:
    a. during the interview
    b. before the interview
    c. after the interview
    d. when your resume is reviewed

Short Answer

26. What are three things you should do when targeting possible employment opportunities?

27. Why is it important to understand different personality styles?

28. What is the difference between gross and net pay?

29. Explain the three basic withholdings on a paycheck stub.

30. Would you do something you did not like in order to make five to ten times more income? Why or why not?

Case Studies

31. Merideth is almost finished with her second year of college where she is majoring in marketing and advertising. She is not excited about her studies lately and has been thinking about switching over to the nursing field. Her income as a nurse will not be as much as what a good advertising firm would pay, and it wouldn't be as glamorous as working on a big account. Merideth does not really want to lose the two years of college she has put in and start over, but she would essentially have to in order to go into nursing. Should Merideth finish out the remaining two years of this degree or make the switch now and start back at square one? Explain your answer.

32. Ryan loves his work, but he is only making enough for him and his pregnant wife to get by. They have no savings set aside and they have $5,000 in credit card debt. His income is only $35,000 per year, but he has now been offered a position making $65,000 per year. He is considering taking the job even though he knows he will eventually hate working at this company. Ryan figures he needs to make as much as possible. What should he do? Why?

33. Alex is a sophomore at a local college. He wants to transfer to a prestigious university. If he does, he would incur more than $50,000 in student loan debt. His parents are against the idea. What would Dave say?

INS and OUTS of INSURANCE

What do other high school students know about insurance?

We asked high school students about what they think about insurance.

> " Insurance is something that will pay for medical help. It's money for any medical problems you will have **now or in the future.**
>
> Junior, Mississippi "

" There are different types of insurance to insure different things like your house or car, and then there is life insurance which will help your family if you die."

Sophomore, Florida

" I know women pay less for insurance and you get a discount if you take drivers education."

Junior, Oklahoma

" Everyone needs life insurance, which some people also call 'death insurance.'"

Senior, Missouri

" Insurance covers liability and protects you. It provides cash for accidental occurrences."

Senior, Florida

LEARNING OUTCOMES

Explain why insurance is an essential part of a healthy financial plan.

Identify and describe the seven basic types of insurance coverage needed.

Understand the importance of disability insurance.

Evaluate the reasons why life insurance is not an investment.

Differentiate between term and cash value life insurance.

List types of insurances to avoid.

KEY TERMS

Cash Value Insurance
Collision
Comprehensive
Disability Insurance
Health Insurance
Renter's Insurance
Term Insurance

BEFORE YOU BEGIN

What do you know about insurance?

Answer the following questions before you watch Dave's lesson. Decide whether each statement is true or false. Then provide a short explanation for why you think a statement is false.

TRUE **FALSE**
☐ ☐

Insurance rates can vary depending on the company, and I can save money if I shop around.

....

....

TRUE **FALSE**
☐ ☐

I always have to have collision insurance on my automobile, even if it is an old car that's not worth much.

....

....

TRUE **FALSE**
☐ ☐

If an employer offers me health insurance but requires me to pay part of the premium, it is not a good deal and I shouldn't get it.

....

....

TRUE **FALSE**
☐ ☐

I only need to have renter's insurance if I have a lot of valuable items.

....

....

TRUE **FALSE**
☐ ☐

Everyone should have life insurance.

....

....

Understanding Insurance

Insurance is an essential financial planning tool.

The purpose of insurance is to _____ risk.

Without proper insurance, certain losses can _____ you. Conventional wisdom says that you should transfer risk.

Basic Types of Coverage Needed

1. Homeowner's or Renter's Insurance

2. Auto Insurance

3. Health Insurance

4. Disability Insurance

5. Long-Term Care Insurance

6. Identity Theft Protection

7. Life Insurance

! STUPID TAX

"My boyfriend bought a car and then wrecked it. Now he has to walk, but he is still paying for that car."

Senior, Alabama

"I bought an expensive CD player for my car and threw the receipt away. I found out that the CD player would not work in my car—it wasn't adaptable."

Senior, New Mexico

"I bought an expensive phone and lost it the next week. It was a big waste of money because I didn't have insurance on it."

Senior, Alabama

"It is unwise to hope for the best without preparing for the worst."

Anonymous

Types of Insurance

Homeowner's and Auto Insurance

If you have a full emergency fund, raise your _____.

Carry adequate liability.

Consider dropping your _____ on older cars.

END OF VIDEO PART 1

Homeowner's insurance should be "guaranteed _____ cost."

_____ liability policies are a good buy once you have some assets.

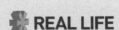

REAL LIFE

Auto insurance is an important part of owning a vehicle and being a responsible driver. But there are a few things you should know to help you find the right insurer, get the most out of your coverage, and protect your interests when filing a claim.

Money Magazine

Top Things to Know About Auto Insurance

1. You're a statistic. To an insurer, you're not a person—you're a set of risks. An insurer bases its decisions on your "risk factors," including some things that may seem unrelated to driving a car.

2. Insurers differ. Prices can vary from company to company. You can save money by comparison shopping.

3. Don't just look at price. A low price is no bargain if an insurer takes forever to service your claim. Research the insurer's record for claims service, as well as its financial stability.

4. Go beyond the basics. Although most states require only a minimum of liability coverage, you should look for a minimum coverage of $500,000.

5. Demand discounts. Insurers provide discounts to reward behavior that reduces risk. However, Americans waste $300 billion a year because they forget to ask for discounts!

6. At claims time, your insurer isn't necessarily your friend. Your idea of fair compensation may not match that of your insurer. Your insurer's job is to restore you financially. Your job is to prove your losses so that you get what you need.

7. Prepare before you have to file a claim. Keep your policy updated and reread it before you file a claim, so there are no surprises.

Health Insurance

Keys to saving on your health premiums:

Increase your _____ and/or coinsurance amount.

Increase your _____ - _____, but never decrease your maximum pay.

See if an _____, a Health Savings Account, would make sense for your situation.

The HSA is a _____ - _____ savings account for medical expenses that works with a high deductible insurance policy. **END OF VIDEO PART 2**

Disability Insurance

Disability insurance is designed to replace _____ lost due to a short-term or permanent disability.

Try to buy disability insurance that pays if you cannot perform the job that you were educated or _____ to do.

That is called _____, or "own occ," disability. Many times, this is only available for two years.

Beware of _____ - term policies covering less than _____ years.

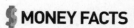

MONEY FACTS

Most auto insurance providers offer up to **25% discounts** for students that maintain a "B" average or better with their grades.

Various companies

47 million Americans do not have health insurance.

National Coalition on Health Care

Young adults (age 18–24) are the **least likely** of any age group to have health insurance.

National Coalition on Health Care

Medical bills and illness are the **number one** cause of bankruptcy in the U.S.

Harvard Study

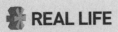 **REAL LIFE**

Things to Remember About Disability Insurance

Disability insurance is a long-term solution. Your short-term needs should be covered by a full emergency fund of three to six months of expenses.

Buy disability with after-tax dollars. If you become disabled and you bought disability insurance with pre-tax dollars, your disability income will be taxable.

Your coverage should be for _____% of your current income.

The _____ period is the time between the disabling event and when the payments actually begin.

A _____ elimination period will _____ your premium cost. ◄ END OF VIDEO PART 3

Long-Term Care Insurance

Long-term care insurance is for _____ home, assisted living facilities or in-home care.

_____% of people over the age of 65 will require long-term care at some point in their lives.

Identity Theft Protection

Don't buy identity theft protection that only provides credit report _____.

Good protection includes _____ services that assign a _____ to clean up the mess. ◄ END OF VIDEO PART 4

Life Insurance

Life insurance is to replace lost income due to _____.

Most people have no _____ what kind of life insurance they _____.

Two Types of Life Insurance

1. _____ insurance is for a specified period, is substantially cheaper, and has no savings plan built into it.

2. _____ _____ insurance is normally for life and is more expensive because it funds a savings plan.

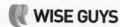 **WISE GUYS**

Human beings have a 100% mortality rate—we're all going to die someday. If people depend on your income, it is your responsibility to make sure they'll be taken care of if something were to happen to you.

"My car was recently totaled, but I had full coverage insurance. The problem is the bank is asking for $3,000 in 30 days because I did not have gap insurance. What is gap insurance? I thought I would finally be done with these car payments because the insurance would take care of everything, but now I have this bill. What can I do?"

DAVE'S ANSWER: Gap insurance covers the difference between what you owe on a car and what the insurance company says it is worth. That is what happened to you. Your full coverage policy paid for the current value of the car, but that is less than what you owe the bank. Since you no longer have the car as collateral, the bank is calling their note.

Gap insurance can be pretty expensive, which is another reason not to buy a new car on credit. The minute you drive off the car lot with a new car, it loses value and if you get into an accident, there will be a gap that you are responsible for unless you have this gap insurance. All you can do right now is pay the bank what you owe and move on, lesson learned.

"What is your opinion on having life insurance on small children?"

DAVE'S ANSWER: I think it's a total waste of money. The only exception may be a small rider on your term insurance policy—just enough to take care of a child's funeral expenses—in the event that something awful happens. I did that for years, just a little $15,000 rider, before I decided to self-insure on that issue.

People usually buy life insurance on kids for two reasons: as an investment and for some misplaced peace of mind. Number one, they should never be used as an investment. They're garbage as investment vehicles. The second reason most people buy life insurance on kids is because they're scared the child may get really sick later on and become uninsurable. The likelihood of that happening is almost zero. That's why it's so inexpensive.

The people with a real need for life insurance are those who have others depending on them for their livelihood. These people should carry about 10 times their annual income on a good, 20-year level term life insurance policy.

The most common insurance myth is that the need for life insurance is a _____ situation.

Twenty years from today, when the children are grown and gone, you are debt-free (including the 15-year mortgage), and you have investments that have grown to a substantial amount, you will have become self-_____.

Why Not Life Insurance as an Investment?

1. Returns are historically _____.

2. When you die with cash value, the insurance company _____ the cash value.

3. The _____ deducted from your return are extremely _____.

Cash Value vs. Term + Roth IRA

Cash value life insurance is a bad investment. Consider this:

For $145 a month, you could have $125,000 in cash value insurance. Or, for that same $145, you could pay $10 for $400,000 in 20-year term insurance and invest $135 into a Roth IRA. If you start at age 30 your investment will be worth...

Age	$125,000 Cash Value GUARANTEED	$135/mo in Roth 12% RETURN
50	$27,500	$133,000
70	$66,000	$1,500,000

Before You Cancel Your Cash Value Policy...

Make sure that you already have a new term policy in place! If, for some reason, you cannot be approved for a new term policy, it is better to hang on to a bad cash value policy than to have nothing at all—until you become self-insured.

What to Remember When Purchasing Life Insurance

REAL LIFE

Some companies will do anything to make a buck—including insurance companies. Here are a few bizarre examples of actual insurance plans available:

• Alien abduction insurance
• Pet insurance
• Wedding insurance
• Body part insurance

1. Buy only low-cost level _____.

2. Do not forget your _____. **END OF VIDEO PART 5**

3. Stay away from fancy _____.

4. Children only need enough for _____ expenses.

5. You need about _____ times your income. Invested at 10-12%, the annual interest would replace your lost income.

Insurance to Avoid

1. _____ life and disability

2. Credit _____ protection

3. _____ and hospital indemnity

4. Accidental _____

5. Any insurance with _____ _____, investments or refunds

6. Pre-paid _____ policies

7. _____ life insurance

8. Any kind of _____ coverage

◀ END OF VIDEO PART 6

Recap and Review

Insurance is not an investment. Its only function is to transfer risk.

You must have auto insurance if you have a car.

Renter's insurance is essential for renters, including when you live in a dorm at college.

Health insurance is important, even if you have to pay more than you would like.

Raising your deductible can save money on your premiums.

Identity theft is on the rise. Guard your personal information at all times and buy identity theft protection that includes restoration services.

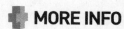
MORE INFO

Cafeteria plan is an employee benefit arrangement allowed by IRS Code Section 125, under which employees are allowed to pay for certain employee benefits on a pretax, rather than an after-tax, basis. Cafeteria plans, also known as Section 125 plans (because of the section of the IRS code that covers them), and flexible benefit plans allow employees to have some choice in designing his or her own benefit package. Cafeteria plans typically have core benefits such as medical and life insurance, sick leave and sometimes disability benefits. Optional benefits may include anything from dental insurance and elder care to vision coverage. They can't, however, include transportation assistance, tuition assistance or, unless part of a 401(k) plan, retirement benefits.

Vocabulary

Auto Insurance
Beneficiary
Break-Even Analysis
Cash Value Insurance
Claim
Collision
Comprehensive
Co-Pay
Coverage
Deductible
Elimination Period
Extended Replacement Cost
Guaranteed Replacement Cost
HSA
Health Insurance
Homeowner's Insurance
Level Term
Liability
Life Insurance
Long-Term Care Insurance
Long-Term Disability
Maximum Payment
Mortgage Insurance
Occupational Disability
Out of Pocket
Permanent Disability
Policy
Premiums
Renter's Insurance
Restoration Services
Self-Insured
Short-Term Disability
Stop-Loss
Term Insurance
Umbrella
Universal Life
Variable Life
Whole Life Insurance

Matching

a. comprehensive
b. collision
c. 10
d. 20
e. premium
f. out of pocket

____ 1. The amount you pay for an insurance policy

____ 2. Costs that insurance doesn't cover; amount you pay

____ 3. The amount of life insurance you should have is ____ times your income

____ 4. Covers damage to a car if there is an accident

____ 5. Covers damage to a car if a tree falls on it

True or False

____ 6. The deductible on any insurance is the portion you have to pay before insurance covers any expenses.

____ 7. If you have an older car, you can consider dropping liability.

____ 8. The purpose of insurance is to transfer risk.

____ 9. Cash value insurance is a good way to invest since it has a savings plan inside it.

____ 10. Neither accidental death nor cancer insurance are good insurance policies to carry.

____ 11. Short-term disability is covered by your emergency fund, so only buy long-term disability.

___ 12. The best type of identity theft insurance only provides credit report monitoring.

Multiple Choice

13. The time between the disabling event and the beginning of payments:
    a. deductible
    b. out of pocket
    c. elimination period
    d. stop gap

14. Life insurance policy for a specific period of time:
    a. term
    b. whole life
    c. universal
    d. level

15. What can you do to decrease the cost of insurance policies?
    a. raise the deductible
    b. shop around for rates
    c. take advantage of applicable discounts
    d. all of the above

Name the Type of Insurance

16. _____ Covers restoration and monitoring services

17. _____ Covers damage to a vehicle

18. _____ Covers the contents of an apartment

19. _____ Designed to replace income lost if you cannot perform your job

20. _____ Covers assisted living, in-home or nursing home care

21. _____ Designed to replace income lost due to death

Short Answer

22. Explain at least two ways you can save on auto insurance.

23. Why do you need renter's insurance if you don't own valuable items?

24. Explain why life insurance is not a good savings plan.

25. When do you need renter's insurance?

Case Studies

26. Sarah's brother sold her a $100,000 whole life insurance policy and she is paying $115 per month in premiums. She is single and has been listening to Dave Ramsey, so she knows that term life insurance would be a better buy. She wants to change but is not sure what to tell her brother. What should she say to him?

27. Bill and Christy have two young children ages two and four, and they are not covered under any life insurance policy. Christy is a full-time mom and has no income. Bill makes $50,000 a year. They are on a budget but with only one income, they do not have any extra money at the end of the month. Life insurance does not seem like a pressing issue at this time. What would you suggest Bill and Christy do when it comes to life insurance coverage?

28. Mark has an older car worth about $5,000. He thinks he is paying too much for auto insurance and wants to find out how he can save. After listening to Dave, Mark decides to look into raising his deductible from $250 to $1,000. By doing this, he can save $65 per year. Is this worth the risk? How long does he have to go without an automobile accident to break even?

REAL ESTATE and MORTGAGES

What do other high school students know about real estate?

We asked high school students to describe their dream home, and tell how they plan to pay for it.

> "My dream house has big windows, white siding, a wraparound porch, a white picket fence, and a view of the ocean. I'll be paying for it in **cold hard cash.**
>
> Junior, Michigan

"My dream house would be out in an open field with blooming wild flowers. I plan to pay for it by getting a well-paying job as a vet tech."

Sophomore, Mississippi

"My dream house is large with extravagant details such as a swimming pool and movie theater. I plan on paying for it by investing."

Senior, Missouri

"It will have 12 bedrooms, 12 baths, a pool, and a balcony that overlooks water on the property. I'm planning to buy it by marrying a rich old man."

Junior, Florida

"The way my life is going, it will be a double-side trailer and I'll be flipping burgers to pay for it."

Freshman, Wyoming

LEARNING OUTCOMES

Describe the steps to take to maximize the sale of a home.

Examine what to look for when purchasing a home.

Evaluate the various types of home mortgages.

Identify the pros and cons of renting versus owning.

Compare and contrast a 15-year mortgage to a 30-year mortgage.

KEY TERMS

ARM
Appraisal
Appreciation
Conventional Loan
Curb Appeal
Equity
Fixed Rate
MLS
Mortgage

BEFORE YOU BEGIN

What do you know about real estate and mortgages?

Before watching the lesson, read each statement below and mark whether you agree or disagree in the "before" column. Then, after watching the lesson, do it again using the "after" column to see if you changed your mind on any question.

Before			After	
Agree	Disagree		Agree	Disagree
☐	☐	1. Your rent or mortgage payment should never be more than 25% of your take-home pay.	☐	☐
☐	☐	2. Always try to purchase a home in the top price range of the neighborhood to maximize appreciation.	☐	☐
☐	☐	3. Since selling a home is much easier now with the Internet, it's a good idea to sell your own home and save money on the real estate agent's commission.	☐	☐
☐	☐	4. ARM and balloon mortgages were made to help consumers combat high interest rates and transfer the risk to the lender.	☐	☐
☐	☐	5. Buying a house is not only a good investment, but it is also a tax advantage. You are better off buying than throwing money away on rent.	☐	☐

What are your initial thoughts about real estate and mortgages?

....
....
....
....
....

What do you want to learn about real estate and mortgages?

....
....
....
....
....

FEEDBACK

"Working and saving up for something makes me think twice before buying it."

Sophomore, Florida

"The more you save, the more you will have for something you really want."

Junior, Michigan

 Pay off your home early.

Selling a Home

When selling a home, you should think like a

_____.

The home should be in "near perfect" condition.

The return on investment of fix-up dollars is _____.

END OF VIDEO PART 1

The most important aspect of preparation is attention to the _____ appeal.

When selling your home, make sure that it is listed on the _____.

When selling, statistical research has found that the best realtors are worth _____ than they cost.

The exposure through the _____ Listing Service (MLS) is worth it.

When selecting a realtor, do not rely on

_____ or _____.

MONEY FACTS

There were **2.2 million** foreclosure filings in the U.S. during 2007.

bizjournals.com

More than **67%** of Americans are homeowners.

U.S. Census Bureau

Subprime mortgages are loans made to borrowers who are perceived to have **high credit risk.**

Federal Reserve

Adjustable Rate Mortgages (ARMs) account for nearly **one-third** of all mortgages.

realestatejournal.com

These are professionals. You should always _____ them.

Offering a home _____ will typically not make a sale. If the buyer asks for a warranty, then consider it with that offer.

Buying a Home

Home ownership is a great investment for three main reasons:

1. It's a _____ savings plan.

2. It's an _____ hedge.

3. It grows virtually _____ - _____.

You can have a gain of $250,000 single or $500,000 married and pay zero tax on the sale of your personal residence if you hold it at least two years.

Title insurance insures you against an _____ title, which is when your proper ownership is in question. It is a good buy.

Always get a land _____ if buying more than a standard subdivision lot.

END OF VIDEO PART 2

Realtors' access to the _____ system can make house hunting easier, but be careful. Many agents can only think like retailers, which is not what you want when buying.

"After college I want to buy land for a farm. What can I do now to be able to pay cash for this when it's time?"

DAVE'S ANSWER: That's an awesome goal! First and foremost you should stay out of debt. Debt is an acid that eats up your income, so stay away from student loan debt and all other kinds of debt. Being debt free greatly increases the amount of money you'll have in your pockets. As you save that money, you'll be able to use it toward your game plan.

Next, start looking in places you might want to buy land and find out how much it will cost. Then decide exactly when you want to buy the land. After this, you'll be able to formulate a plan detailing exactly how much you'll need to save during college and right after graduation. Breaking down large purchases like this into a step by step process makes it easier.

What to Buy

Buy in the _____ price range of the neighborhood.

Homes appreciate in good neighborhoods and are priced based on three things: _____, _____, and _____!

If possible, buy near _____ or with a _____.

Buy bargains by _____ bad landscaping, outdated carpet, ugly wallpaper and the ELVIS print in the master bedroom. **END OF VIDEO PART 3**

However…

Always buy a home that is (or can be) attractive from the _____ and has a good basic _____.

REAL LIFE

Buying Your First Home

The ONLY time you should buy a home is when you are out of debt and have a full emergency fund (3-6 months of expenses) saved up. You should also have a 20% down payment saved so you won't have to pay private mortgage insurance. Now, you may be saying "If I wait until I'm out of debt, I'll be throwing a lot of money away on rent." When you think that, remember this: if you have debt, no savings and move into a house, Murphy will move in your spare bedroom. If you move into a home and something breaks, you won't have the money to fix it. So you'll borrow the money to fix it and take on more debt. If you get gazelle-intense about getting out of debt, make a budget and maybe work an extra job, it won't be long before you're debt-free and have money in the bank. Then you are ready to start house shopping.

Have the home inspected mechanically and structurally by a certified _____ _____.

Appraisals are an "_____ of value," but it's a better opinion than the current homeowner has. Always order one if in doubt.

What Not to Buy

1. _____ or _____ _____

2. _____

Mortgages

First, remember to _____ debt.

The best mortgage is the _____ down plan.

But if you must get a mortgage...

Do not buy until you are ready. That means you are out of debt with a fully-funded emergency fund.

There is nothing wrong with _____ for a little while. This demonstrates _____ and wisdom.

Get a payment of no more than _____ of your take home pay on a _____ fixed-rate loan, with at least _____ down.

Have a fully-funded emergency fund left over after closing.

END OF VIDEO PART 4

 **MORE INFO**

Private Mortgage Insurance (PMI) is extra insurance that lenders require from most home buyers who do not have a 20 % down payment when they buy a home and take out a mortgage.

How Much Will You Save?
30 Year vs. 15 Year Mortgage at 6%

			PAYMENT	TOTAL	PAY BACK
Home Purchased	$250,000	30 years	$1,349	$485,636
Down Payment	$ 25,000	15 years	$1,899	$341,762
Mortgage Amount	$225,000	Difference	$ 550	$143,874

You save more than $143,000!

Horrible Mortgage Options

1. Adjustable Rate Mortgages (ARM) were brought on with the advent of _____ interest rates in the early 1980's.

▶ The concept of the ARM is to _____ the risk of higher interest rates to the _____ and, in return, the lender gives a lower rate up front.

▶ Of course, _____ _____ loans are a bad idea because you are only paying the interest.

▶ You can qualify for more home with ARMs, but the risk of financial stress later is not worth it.

WISE GUYS

"A man builds a fine house; and now he has a master, and a task for life; he is to furnish, watch, show it, and keep it in repair the rest of his days."

Ralph Waldo Emerson

2. _____ Mortgages

▶ Bad idea because you are putting a paid-for home at risk and the fees are horrible.

3. _____, or Bi-Weekly Payoff

▶ Allows you to make a half-payment every two weeks, which equals 13 payments a year. The reason it pays off early is because you make one extra payment a year.

▶ Do not pay a fee for this option. You can easily do this on your own.

Where's the Tax Advantage?

Mortgage Amount	Interest Rate	Annual Interest Paid
$200,000	**5%**	**$10,000**

Mortgage interest is tax-deductible, so you would not have to pay taxes on this $10,000. That is why many people tell you to keep the mortgage. But what does this really save you?

Taxable Amount	Tax Bracket	Annual Taxes Paid
$10,000	**25%**	**$2,500**

So, if you keep your mortgage just for the "tax advantages," all you are really doing is sending $10,000 to the bank instead of sending $2,500 to the IRS. Where's the *advantage* in that?

> "I am 23 years old and just got married this year. My wife and I owe $15,000 on our cars and we are renting a small apartment. We are wondering if we should buy a house, with small payments of course, as a good investment?"

DAVE'S ANSWER: You have to get your cars totally paid off, as well as any other debt you have, and have a 3-6 month emergency fund set up. I'm a fan of real estate, but I think most couples make impulsive decisions in their first year of marriage about owning versus renting. They listen to young—and not so bright—people they know that are going out and buying houses and furniture on credit. This is a dumb idea.

I would rent for your first few years, get out of debt, get an emergency fund, and make a huge down payment. A house can turn into a curse if you can't afford the upkeep and all the stuff that goes along with owning a house. Emergency funds are Murphy repellent, and you are going to want some of that when you buy a house.

4. _____ Advantages of a Mortgage

▸ Do not fall for the myth that you should keep your mortgage for the tax advantages. The math doesn't work.

Basic Ways to Finance A Home

1. _____, usually through the Federal National Mortgage Association (FNMA) and privately insured against default.

▸ Down payments range from 5% to 20% or more.

! STUPID TAX

"I buy all the $1 deals that I can find and never use them."

Junior, Oklahoma

"I paid $100 for a pair of designer jeans at the mall when I could have gotten a couple pairs of cheaper jeans and had more clothes to wear."

Senior, Alabama

▶ These loans are available in all forms and formats.

▶ PMI is _____ mortgage insurance.

2. _____, which is insured by the U.S. Department of Housing and Urban Development (HUD)—the federal government.

   ▶ Down payments are as low as _____ and are used on lower-priced homes.

   ▶ These loans are currently _____ expensive than conventional financing and should be avoided.

3. _____, which is insured by the Veterans Administration (VA).

   ▶ Designed to benefit the veteran; the seller pays everything allowing for a true zero-down purchase.

   ▶ With a good down payment, the conventional loan is a _____ deal.

4. _____ financing is when you pay the owner over time, making him/her the mortgage holder.

   ▶ This is a _____ way to finance because you can be creative in the structure of the loan.

Example: No payments for a year, interest rates that graduate, or discount for early payoff. **END OF VIDEO PART 5**

Recap and Review

Your rent or house payment should never be more than 25% of your take-home pay.

Always work through a good realtor and make sure to have the home inspected.

Stay away from adjustable rate mortgages and interest only loans.

If you must take out a mortgage, do not do so until you have a fully-funded emergency fund, you are debt free, and you have at least a 10% down payment. (20% to avoid paying PMI.)

Vocabulary

Accelerated Payment
Appraisal
Appreciation
ARM
Conventional Loan
Curb Appeal
Equity
FHA Loan
Fixed Rate
Home Inspector
Home Warranty
Inflation Hedge
Interest Only Loan
Land Survey
MLS
Mortgage
Owner Financing
PMI
Principal
Realtor
Reverse Mortgage
Timeshare
Title Insurance
VA Loan

Matching

a. mortgage
b. equity
c. principal
d. MLS
e. title insurance
f. home warranty
g. land survey
h. appreciation

____ 1. The value of your house over and above the mortgage

____ 2. Listing service realtors use

____ 3. Protects you against an ownership claim

____ 4. Loan secured by collateral of a specific real estate property

____ 5. Shows where property lines are

____ 6. The face value of your mortgage, not including interest

____ 7. An increase in value

____ 8. An agreement that ensures the structural soundness of a home

True or False

Determine whether these statements are true or false. Change the false statements to read true.

_____ 9. Baby Step 7 is to pay off your house.

_____

_____

_____

_____ 10. The best mortgage is an adjustable rate mortgage.

_____

_____

_____

_____ 11. A real estate agent is usually well worth the commission.

_____

_____

_____

_____ 12. Friends or relatives make the best real estate agents.

_____

_____

_____

_____ 13. Your rent or mortgage payment should be at least 25% or more of your take-home pay.

_____

_____

_____

Multiple Choice

14. What type of mortgage is an ARM?
    a. advanced rate mortgage
    b. adjustable rate mortgage
    c. American Realtor Mortgage
    d. none of the above

15. Which is not a type of mortgage?
    a. reverse
    b. Veterans Administration
    c. lease to own
    d. conventional

16. Which is not an investment benefit to home ownership?
    a. lower tax bracket
    b. grows virtually tax free
    c. inflation hedge
    d. forced savings plan

17. How much do you need for a down payment in order to avoid paying PMI?
    a. 0%
    b. 10%
    c. 20%
    d. 50%

18. Which is true about owner financing?
    a. the buyer makes payments to the owner
    b. you can be creative in structuring the terms of the loan
    c. you can include a discount for early payoff
    d. all of the above

Short Answer

19. Describe two things you can do to get a home ready to sell.

20. Why is a good realtor worth the money you pay in commission?

21. What are three reasons why home ownership is a great investment?

22. What conditions need to be in place before you buy a house?

23. Explain why people take out ARM or balloon mortgages.

24. What are the benefits to having at least a 20% down payment?

25. Outline the differences between a conventional, VA and FHA loan.

Case Studies

26. Jocelyn and Derrick are engaged to be married in three months and have found their dream home. They have the option of getting a conventional loan or a VA loan. If they take the conventional loan, they need a 5% down payment. If they take the VA loan, they can move in with nothing down. Jocelyn and Derrick have the money for the down payment on the conventional loan, but they wish to buy some furniture and other items they need. Derrick, being a veteran, thinks he should take advantage of the VA loan. What is Dave's advice to them?

27. Blake and Sarah are looking into an adjustable rate mortgage as a financing option. They have found a house they like, but will barely be able to make the payments on a fixed interest rate. With the ARM, they are sure they can make the payments. By the time the rate increases, Blake and Sarah believe they will have both received raises at work. Then, they will change over to a fixed rate on a 30-year mortgage. Whenever they get a bonus, they will apply it to the loan. Blake and Sarah are tired of renting and are anxious to buy this house. What is Dave's advice?

28. Laura and George are both 23 and ready to buy their first home. Combined, their take home pay is about $4,000 a month and they have no debt. What is the maximum amount they should have for a house payment even though they would qualify for a much larger loan amount?

STUDENT RESOURCES

PERSONAL FINANCE FORMS

GLOSSARY

FORMS

Basic Student Budget

ITEM	MONTHLY TOTAL	ACCOUNT
GIVING	_____	_____
SAVING	_____	_____
HOUSING		
Rent	_____	_____
Rental Insurance	_____	_____
UTILITIES		
Cell Phone	_____	_____
Food	_____	_____
Electric	_____	_____
Cable	_____	_____
Internet	_____	_____
TRANSPORTATION		
Car Payment	_____	_____
Gas	_____	_____
Oil Change	_____	_____
Repairs & Tires	_____	_____
Car Insurance	_____	_____
CLOTHING	_____	_____
PERSONAL		
Health Insurance	_____	_____
Entertainment	_____	_____
OTHER MISC.	_____	_____
TOTAL MONTHLY NECESSITIES	_____	

Major Components of a Healthy Financial Plan

	ACTION NEEDED	ACTION DATE
Written Cash Flow Plan	_____	_____
Will and/or Estate Plan	_____	_____
Debt Reduction Plan	_____	_____
Tax Reduction Plan	_____	_____
Emergency Funding	_____	_____
Retirement Funding	_____	_____
College Funding	_____	_____
Charitable Giving	_____	_____
Teach My Children	_____	_____
Life Insurance	_____	_____
Health Insurance	_____	_____
Disability Insurance	_____	_____
Auto Insurance	_____	_____
Homeowner's Insurance	_____	_____

I, _____, a responsible adult, do hereby
promise to take the above stated actions by the above stated dates to financially
secure the well-being of my (our) family and myself (ourselves).

Signed:_____ Date:_____

Signed:_____ Date:_____

Consumer Equity Sheet

ITEM / DESCRIBE	VALUE	-	DEBT	=	EQUITY
Real Estate _____	_____		_____		_____
Real Estate _____	_____		_____		_____
Car _____	_____		_____		_____
Car _____	_____		_____		_____
Cash On Hand	_____		_____		_____
Checking Account	_____		_____		_____
Checking Account	_____		_____		_____
Savings Account	_____		_____		_____
Savings Account	_____		_____		_____
Money Market Account	_____		_____		_____
Mutual Funds	_____		_____		_____
Retirement Plan	_____		_____		_____
Cash Value (Insurance)	_____		_____		_____
Household Items	_____		_____		_____
Jewelry	_____		_____		_____
Antiques	_____		_____		_____
Boat	_____		_____		_____
Unsecured Debt (Neg)	_____		_____		_____
Credit Card Debt (Neg)	_____		_____		_____
Other _____	_____		_____		_____
Other _____	_____		_____		_____
Other _____	_____		_____		_____
TOTAL	_____		_____		_____

Income Sources

SOURCE	AMOUNT	PERIOD/DESCRIBE
Salary 1	_____	_____
Salary 2	_____	_____
Salary 3	_____	_____
Bonus	_____	_____
Self-Employment	_____	_____
Interest Income	_____	_____
Dividend Income	_____	_____
Royalty Income	_____	_____
Rents	_____	_____
Notes	_____	_____
Alimony	_____	_____
Child Support	_____	_____
AFDC	_____	_____
Unemployment	_____	_____
Social Security	_____	_____
Pension	_____	_____
Annuity	_____	_____
Disability Income	_____	_____
Cash Gifts	_____	_____
Trust Fund	_____	_____
Other_____	_____	_____
Other_____	_____	_____
Other_____	_____	_____
TOTAL	_____	

Lump Sum Payment Planning

ITEM NEEDED	ANNUAL AMOUNT		MONTHLY AMOUNT
Real Estate Taxes	_____	/ 12 =	_____
Homeowner's Insurance	_____	/ 12 =	_____
Home Repairs	_____	/ 12 =	_____
Replace Furniture	_____	/ 12 =	_____
Medical Bills	_____	/ 12 =	_____
Health Insurance	_____	/ 12 =	_____
Life Insurance	_____	/ 12 =	_____
Disability Insurance	_____	/ 12 =	_____
Car Insurance	_____	/ 12 =	_____
Car Repair/Tags	_____	/ 12 =	_____
Replace Car	_____	/ 12 =	_____
Clothing	_____	/ 12 =	_____
Tuition	_____	/ 12 =	_____
Bank Note	_____	/ 12 =	_____
IRS (Self-Employed)	_____	/ 12 =	_____
Vacation	_____	/ 12 =	_____
Gifts (including Christmas)	_____	/ 12 =	_____
Other _____	_____	/ 12 =	_____

Recommended Percentages

ITEM	ACTUAL %	RECOMMENDED %
Charitable Gifts	_____	10 – 15%
Saving	_____	5 – 10%
Housing	_____	25 – 35%
Utilities	_____	5 – 10%
Food	_____	5 – 15%
Transportation	_____	10 – 15%
Clothing	_____	2 – 7%
Medical/Health	_____	5 – 10%
Personal	_____	5 – 10%
Recreation	_____	5 – 10%
Debts	_____	5 – 10%

Monthly Cash Flow Plan

BUDGETED ITEM	SUB TOTAL	TOTAL	ACTUALLY SPENT	% OF TAKE HOME PAY
CHARITABLE GIFTS	_____		_____	_____
SAVING				
Emergency Fund	_____		_____	
Retirement Fund	_____			
College Fund	_____	_____	_____	_____
HOUSING				
First Mortgage	_____		_____	
Second Mortgage	_____		_____	
Real Estate Taxes	_____		_____	
Homeowner's Ins.	_____		_____	
Repairs or Mn. Fee	_____		_____	
Replace Furniture	_____		_____	
Other _____	_____	_____	_____	_____
UTILITIES				
Electricity	_____		_____	
Water	_____		_____	
Gas	_____		_____	
Phone	_____		_____	
Trash	_____		_____	
Cable	_____	_____	_____	_____
*FOOD				
*Groceries	_____		_____	
*Restaurants	_____	_____	_____	_____
TRANSPORTATION				
Car Payment	_____		_____	
Car Payment	_____		_____	
*Gas and Oil	_____		_____	
*Repairs and Tires	_____		_____	
Car Insurance	_____		_____	
License and Taxes	_____		_____	
Car Replacement	_____	_____	_____	
PAGE 1 TOTAL		_____	_____	

Monthly Cash Flow Plan (Continued)

BUDGETED ITEM	SUB TOTAL	TOTAL	ACTUALLY SPENT	% OF TAKE HOME PAY
*CLOTHING				
*Children	_____		_____	
*Adults	_____		_____	
*Cleaning/Laundry	_____	_____	_____	_____
MEDICAL/HEALTH				
Disability Insurance	_____		_____	
Health Insurance	_____		_____	
Doctor Bills	_____		_____	
Dentist	_____		_____	
Optometrist	_____		_____	
Medications	_____	_____	_____	_____
PERSONAL				
Life Insurance	_____		_____	
Child Care	_____		_____	
*Baby Sitter	_____		_____	
*Toiletries	_____		_____	
*Cosmetics	_____		_____	
*Hair Care	_____		_____	
Education/Adult	_____		_____	
School Tuition	_____		_____	
School Supplies	_____		_____	
Child Support	_____		_____	
Alimony	_____		_____	
Subscriptions	_____		_____	
Organization Dues	_____		_____	
Gifts (incl. Christmas)	_____		_____	
Miscellaneous	_____		_____	
*Blow Money	_____	_____	_____	_____
PAGE 2 TOTAL		_____	_____	

Monthly Cash Flow Plan (Continued)

BUDGETED ITEM	SUB TOTAL	TOTAL	ACTUALLY SPENT	% OF TAKE HOME PAY
RECREATION				
*Entertainment	_____		_____	
Vacation	_____	_____	_____	_____
DEBTS (Hopefully None)				
Visa 1	_____		_____	
Visa 2	_____		_____	
Master Card 1	_____		_____	
Master Card 2	_____		_____	
American Express	_____		_____	
Discover Card	_____		_____	
Gas Card 1	_____		_____	
Gas Card 2	_____		_____	
Dept. Store Card 1	_____		_____	
Dept. Store Card 2	_____		_____	
Finance Co. 1	_____		_____	
Finance Co. 2	_____		_____	
Credit Line	_____		_____	
Student Loan 1	_____		_____	
Student Loan 2	_____		_____	
Other _____	_____		_____	
Other _____	_____		_____	
Other _____	_____		_____	
Other _____	_____		_____	
Other _____	_____	_____	_____	_____
PAGE 3 TOTAL		_____	_____	
PAGE 2 TOTAL		_____	_____	
PAGE 1 TOTAL		_____	_____	
GRAND TOTAL		_____	_____	
TOTAL HOUSEHOLD INCOME		_____		
		ZERO		

Allocated Spending Plan

PAY PERIOD: ____ / ____   ____ / ____   ____ / ____   ____ / ____

ITEM:
INCOME ____ / ____   ____ / ____   ____ / ____   ____ / ____

CHARITABLE ____ / ____   ____ / ____   ____ / ____   ____ / ____

SAVING

Emergency Fund ____ / ____   ____ / ____   ____ / ____   ____ / ____
Retirement Fund ____ / ____   ____ / ____   ____ / ____   ____ / ____
College Fund ____ / ____   ____ / ____   ____ / ____   ____ / ____

HOUSING

First Mortgage ____ / ____   ____ / ____   ____ / ____   ____ / ____
Second Mortgage ____ / ____   ____ / ____   ____ / ____   ____ / ____
Real Estate Taxes ____ / ____   ____ / ____   ____ / ____   ____ / ____
Homeowner's Ins. ____ / ____   ____ / ____   ____ / ____   ____ / ____
Repairs or Mn. Fees ____ / ____   ____ / ____   ____ / ____   ____ / ____
Replace Furniture ____ / ____   ____ / ____   ____ / ____   ____ / ____
Other _____ ____ / ____   ____ / ____   ____ / ____   ____ / ____

UTILITIES

Electricity ____ / ____   ____ / ____   ____ / ____   ____ / ____
Water ____ / ____   ____ / ____   ____ / ____   ____ / ____
Gas ____ / ____   ____ / ____   ____ / ____   ____ / ____
Phone ____ / ____   ____ / ____   ____ / ____   ____ / ____
Trash ____ / ____   ____ / ____   ____ / ____   ____ / ____
Cable ____ / ____   ____ / ____   ____ / ____   ____ / ____

*FOOD

*Groceries ____ / ____   ____ / ____   ____ / ____   ____ / ____
*Restaurants ____ / ____   ____ / ____   ____ / ____   ____ / ____

Allocated Spending Plan (Continued)

TRANSPORTATION
Car Payment _____ / _____   _____ / _____   _____ / _____   _____ / _____
Car Payment _____ / _____   _____ / _____   _____ / _____   _____ / _____
*Gas and Oil _____ / _____   _____ / _____   _____ / _____   _____ / _____
*Repairs and Tires _____ / _____   _____ / _____   _____ / _____   _____ / _____
Car Insurance _____ / _____   _____ / _____   _____ / _____   _____ / _____
License and Taxes _____ / _____   _____ / _____   _____ / _____   _____ / _____
Car Replacement _____ / _____   _____ / _____   _____ / _____   _____ / _____

*CLOTHING
*Children _____ / _____   _____ / _____   _____ / _____   _____ / _____
*Adults _____ / _____   _____ / _____   _____ / _____   _____ / _____
*Cleaning/Laundry _____ / _____   _____ / _____   _____ / _____   _____ / _____

MEDICAL/HEALTH
Disability Insurance _____ / _____   _____ / _____   _____ / _____   _____ / _____
Health Insurance _____ / _____   _____ / _____   _____ / _____   _____ / _____
Doctor _____ / _____   _____ / _____   _____ / _____   _____ / _____
Dentist _____ / _____   _____ / _____   _____ / _____   _____ / _____
Optometrist _____ / _____   _____ / _____   _____ / _____   _____ / _____
Medications _____ / _____   _____ / _____   _____ / _____   _____ / _____

PERSONAL
Life Insurance _____ / _____   _____ / _____   _____ / _____   _____ / _____
Child Care _____ / _____   _____ / _____   _____ / _____   _____ / _____
*Baby Sitter _____ / _____   _____ / _____   _____ / _____   _____ / _____
*Toiletries _____ / _____   _____ / _____   _____ / _____   _____ / _____
*Cosmetics _____ / _____   _____ / _____   _____ / _____   _____ / _____
*Hair Care _____ / _____   _____ / _____   _____ / _____   _____ / _____
Education/Adult _____ / _____   _____ / _____   _____ / _____   _____ / _____
School Tuition _____ / _____   _____ / _____   _____ / _____   _____ / _____
School Supplies _____ / _____   _____ / _____   _____ / _____   _____ / _____
Child Support _____ / _____   _____ / _____   _____ / _____   _____ / _____

Allocated Spending Plan (Continued)

Alimony ____/____ ____/____ ____/____ ____/____
Subscriptions ____/____ ____/____ ____/____ ____/____
Organization Dues ____/____ ____/____ ____/____ ____/____
Gifts (including Christmas) ____/____ ____/____ ____/____ ____/____
Miscellaneous ____/____ ____/____ ____/____ ____/____

*BLOW MONEY ____/____ ____/____ ____/____ ____/____

RECREATION
*Entertainment ____/____ ____/____ ____/____ ____/____
Vacation ____/____ ____/____ ____/____ ____/____

DEBTS (Hopefully None)
Visa 1 ____/____ ____/____ ____/____ ____/____
Visa 2 ____/____ ____/____ ____/____ ____/____
MasterCard 1 ____/____ ____/____ ____/____ ____/____
MasterCard 2 ____/____ ____/____ ____/____ ____/____
American Express ____/____ ____/____ ____/____ ____/____
Discover Card ____/____ ____/____ ____/____ ____/____
Gas Card 1 ____/____ ____/____ ____/____ ____/____
Gas Card 2 ____/____ ____/____ ____/____ ____/____
Dept. Store Card 1 ____/____ ____/____ ____/____ ____/____
Dept. Store Card 2 ____/____ ____/____ ____/____ ____/____
Finance Co. 1 ____/____ ____/____ ____/____ ____/____
Finance Co. 2 ____/____ ____/____ ____/____ ____/____
Credit Line ____/____ ____/____ ____/____ ____/____
Student Loan 1 ____/____ ____/____ ____/____ ____/____
Student Loan 2 ____/____ ____/____ ____/____ ____/____
Other _____ ____/____ ____/____ ____/____ ____/____
Other _____ ____/____ ____/____ ____/____ ____/____

Irregular Income Planning

ITEM	AMOUNT	CUMULATIVE AMOUNT
_____	_____	_____
_____	_____	_____
_____	_____	_____
_____	_____	_____
_____	_____	_____
_____	_____	_____
_____	_____	_____
_____	_____	_____
_____	_____	_____
_____	_____	_____
_____	_____	_____
_____	_____	_____
_____	_____	_____
_____	_____	_____

Sample Creditor Letter

Date _____

From _____

_____

_____

To _____

_____

_____

RE: _____

Dear _____,

I am writing to formally request that, in accordance with the 1977 Federal Fair Debt Collection Practices Act, your firm (or any agency hired by your firm) no longer contact me at my place of employment, _____.

Please take note that this letter was mailed certified mail, return receipt requested, so that I will have proof that you are in receipt of this letter should legal action against you become necessary.

I am willing to pay the debt I owe you, and I will be in touch with you soon to work out arrangements.

Feel free to contact me at my home between _____ a.m. and _____ p.m. at the following number: _____, or by mail at my home address: _____.

Please give this matter your immediate attention.

Sincerely,

_____

(Signature)

Breakdown of Savings

ITEM	BALANCE BY MONTH		
	_____	_____	_____
Emergency Fund (1) $1,000	_____	_____	_____
Emergency Fund (2) 3-6 months	_____	_____	_____
Retirement Fund	_____	_____	_____
College Fund	_____	_____	_____
Real Estate Taxes	_____	_____	_____
Homeowner's Insurance	_____	_____	_____
Repairs or Mn. Fee	_____	_____	_____
Replace Furniture	_____	_____	_____
Car Insurance	_____	_____	_____
Car Replacement	_____	_____	_____
Disability Insurance	_____	_____	_____
Health Insurance	_____	_____	_____
Doctor	_____	_____	_____
Dentist	_____	_____	_____
Optometrist	_____	_____	_____
Life Insurance	_____	_____	_____
School Tuition	_____	_____	_____
School Supplies	_____	_____	_____
Gifts (incl. Christmas)	_____	_____	_____
Vacation	_____	_____	_____
Other _____	_____	_____	_____
Other _____	_____	_____	_____
TOTAL	_____	_____	_____

Debt Snowball

ITEM	TOTAL PAYOFF	MINIMUM PAYMENT	NEW PAYMENT
_____	_____	_____	_____
_____	_____	_____	_____
_____	_____	_____	_____
_____	_____	_____	_____
_____	_____	_____	_____
_____	_____	_____	_____
_____	_____	_____	_____
_____	_____	_____	_____
_____	_____	_____	_____
_____	_____	_____	_____
_____	_____	_____	_____
_____	_____	_____	_____
_____	_____	_____	_____
_____	_____	_____	_____
_____	_____	_____	_____
_____	_____	_____	_____
_____	_____	_____	_____
_____	_____	_____	_____
_____	_____	_____	_____

Pro Rata Debt List

Income   _____

Necessity Expense   −   _____

Disposable Income   =   _____

Total Debt: _____

Total Monthly Payments: _____

ITEM	TOTAL PAYOFF	/	TOTAL DEBT	=	PERCENT	X	DISPOSABLE INCOME	=	NEW PAYMENT
_____	_____	/	_____	=	_____	X	_____	=	_____
_____	_____	/	_____	=	_____	X	_____	=	_____
_____	_____	/	_____	=	_____	X	_____	=	_____
_____	_____	/	_____	=	_____	X	_____	=	_____
_____	_____	/	_____	=	_____	X	_____	=	_____
_____	_____	/	_____	=	_____	X	_____	=	_____
_____	_____	/	_____	=	_____	X	_____	=	_____
_____	_____	/	_____	=	_____	X	_____	=	_____
_____	_____	/	_____	=	_____	X	_____	=	_____
_____	_____	/	_____	=	_____	X	_____	=	_____
_____	_____	/	_____	=	_____	X	_____	=	_____
_____	_____	/	_____	=	_____	X	_____	=	_____
_____	_____	/	_____	=	_____	X	_____	=	_____
_____	_____	/	_____	=	_____	X	_____	=	_____
_____	_____	/	_____	=	_____	X	_____	=	_____
_____	_____	/	_____	=	_____	X	_____	=	_____
_____	_____	/	_____	=	_____	X	_____	=	_____
_____	_____	/	_____	=	_____	X	_____	=	_____

Monthly Retirement Planning

Too many people use the READY-FIRE-AIM approach to retirement planning. That's a bad plan. You need to aim first. Your assignment is to determine how much per month you should be saving at 12% interest in order to retire at 65 with the amount you need.

If you save at 12% and inflation is at 4%, then you are moving ahead of inflation at a net of 8% per year. If you invest your nest egg at retirement at 12% and want to break even with 4% inflation, you will be living on 8% income.

Step 1: Annual income (today) you wish to retire on: _____

Divide by .08

(Nest egg needed) equals: _____

Step 2: To achieve that nest egg you will save at 12%, netting 8% after inflation. So, we will target that nest egg using 8%.

Nest Egg Needed $ _____

Multiply by 8% Factor   X _____

Monthly Savings Needed   = _____

Note:
Be sure to try one or two examples if you wait 5 or 10 years to start.

8% Factors (select the one that matches your age)		
Your Age	Years to Save	Factor
15	50	.000126
20	45	.000190
25	40	.000286
30	35	.000436
35	30	.000671
40	25	.001051
45	20	.001698
50	15	.002890
55	10	.005466
60	5	.013610

Monthly College Planning

In order to have enough for college, you must aim at something. Your assignment is to determine how much per month you should be saving at 12% interest in order to have enough for college.

If you save at 12% and inflation is at 4%, then you are moving ahead of inflation at a net of 8% per year.

Step 1: In today's dollars, the annual cost of the college of your choice is:

Amount per year $ _____

X 4 years = $ _____

(Hint: $15,000 to $25,000 annually)

Step 2: To achieve that savings you will save at 12%, netting 8% after inflation. So, we will target that by using 8%.

College Savings Needed $ _____

Multiply by Factor   X _____

Monthly Savings Needed   = _____

Note:
Be sure to try one or two examples if you wait 5 or 10 years to start.

8% Factors
(select the one that matches your child's age)

Child's Age	Years to Save	Factor
0	18	.002083
2	16	.002583
4	14	.003287
6	12	.004158
8	10	.005466
10	8	.007470
12	6	.010867
14	4	.017746

Credit Card History

CARD NAME	NUMBER	ADDRESS	PHONE #	CLOSED	WRITTEN CONFIRMATION REQUESTED	WRITTEN CONFIRMATION RECEIVED
Visa	1234 567989 12	1234 Poplar Grove, suite 130	123-456-7890	09/21/06	09/21/06	11/21/06

Insurance Coverage Recap

TYPE	COMPANY	PLAN ID#	POLICY #	AMOUNT	AGENT	PHONE #
Term life	ABC Insurance	1234 561989 12	1234 561989 12	$450,000	John Smith	456-7890

GLOSSARY

401(k): defined contribution plan offered by a corporation to its employees, which allows employees to set aside tax-deferred income for retirement purposes; in some cases, employers will match their contributions.

403(b): retirement plan similar to a 401(k) plan, but one that is offered by non-profit organizations, such as hospitals, schools, and some charitable organizations, rather than corporations; employees set aside tax-deferred dollars.

457 plan: non-qualified, deferred compensation plan established by state and local governments for tax-exempt government agencies and tax-exempt employers; eligible employees are allowed to make salary deferral contributions to the 457 plan; earnings grow on a tax-deferred basis and contributions are not taxed until the assets are distributed from the plan.

529 plan: college savings plan that allows individuals to save on a tax-deferred basis in order to fund future college and graduate school expenses of a child or beneficiary; generally sponsored by a state, these are professionally managed investments.

12b-1 Fee: An annual fee that some mutual funds charge to pay for marketing and distribution activities.

A

Accelerated Payment: making bi-weekly payments on your mortgage which makes one additional payment on your mortgage annually.

Active: money is very active…it is always moving and can be utilized in many ways.

Adjustable Rate Mortgage (ARM): home loan secured by a deed of trust or mortgage in which the interest rate will change periodically (i.e. annually); typically adjusted based on a published index such as the Treasury Bill or LIBOR; brought on as a result of high interest rates in the early 1980s as a way for banks to transfer the risk of higher interest rates to the consumer.

Aggressive Growth Stock Mutual Fund: mutual fund that seeks to provide maximum long-term capital growth from stocks of primarily smaller companies or narrow market segments; dividend income is incidental; the most volatile fund; also referred to as a small-cap fund.

Allowance: money given to a child by his/her parent/guardian, typically on a weekly basis.

Ambition: one's goals and desires in life (i.e., career goals).

Amoral: lacking morals; neither good nor bad.

Amortization Table: breakdown showing how much of each regular payment will be applied toward principal and how much toward interest over the life of a loan; also shows the gradual decrease of the loan balance until it reaches zero.

Annuity: contract sold by an insurance company, designed to provide payments to the holder at specified intervals, usually after retirement; the holder is taxed at the time of distribution or withdrawal, making this a tax-deferred arrangement.

Annual Fee: fee charged by a credit card company for the use of their credit card.

Annual Percentage Rate (APR): cost of borrowing money on an annual basis; takes into account the interest rate and other related fees on a loan.

Appraisal: an opinion of value.

Appreciation: an increase in value.

Asset: anything that is owned by an individual; with respect to saving and investing, assets are generally categorized as liquid (cash) and capital (investment) assets.

Asset Allocation: the process of deciding how investment dollars will be apportioned among various classes of financial assets, such as stocks, bonds and cash investments.

Asset Classes: major categories of financial assets or securities. The three primary classes are common stocks, bonds and cash investments.

ATM card: automated teller card which allows you to make transactions in automated teller machines.

Auctions: a public sale in which property or items of merchandise are sold to the highest bidder.

Auto Insurance: insurance to protect a car owner in the event of an accident or damage to a vehicle.

Average Annual Return: the rate of return on investments averaged over a specific period of time. It is determined by adding together the rates of return for each year and dividing by the number of years in the calculation.

B

Baby Steps: the seven steps to a healthy financial plan.

Back-End Load: sales commission paid when the investor sells mutual fund shares; sometimes phased out over several years; also called redemption fee or contingent-deferred sales charge.

Balanced Fund: mutual fund that invests in more than one type of financial asset: stocks, bonds, and in some cases, cash investments.

Balloon Mortgage: home loan in which the sum of the monthly payments is insufficient to repay the entire loan; a final payment comes due, which is a lump sum of the remaining principal balance.

Bankruptcy: legal procedure for dealing with debt problems of individuals and businesses; specifically a legal court case filed under one of the chapters of Title 11 of the United States Code (also see Chapter 7 bankruptcy, Chapter 11 bankruptcy, and Chapter 13 bankruptcy).

Bargain: deals obtained when negotiating and paying a lesser price than asked for an item.

Beneficiary: the recipient of assets passed on from the death of a friend or relative.

Bond: debt instrument where an issuer such as a corporation, municipality or government agency owes you money; a form of I.O.U.; the issuer makes regular interest payments on the bond and promises to pay back or redeem the face value of the bond at a specified point in the future (the maturity date).

Bond Mutual Fund: mutual funds that buy bonds.

Break-Even Analysis: method used to evaluate the wisdom of a financial decision by determining the length of time it will take for the cost of the decision to be recouped.

Budget: cash flow plan; assigns every dollar to a specific category/expense at the beginning of each month.

Buyer's Remorse: regretting a purchase soon after making it.

C

Capital Gain: a positive difference between an asset's price when bought and its price when sold; the opposite of capital loss.

Capital Gains Distribution: payment to mutual fund shareholders of any gains realized during the year on securities that have been sold at a profit. Capital gains are distributed on a "net" basis after subtracting any capital losses for the year. When losses exceed gains for the year, the difference may be carried forward and subtracted from future gains.

Capital Loss: a negative difference between an asset's price when bought and its price when sold; the opposite of capital gain.

Career: your line of work.

Cash Investments: investments in interest-bearing bank deposits, money market instruments and U.S. Treasury Bills or notes.

Cash Value Insurance: also known as permanent life insurance; premiums include a death benefit and a plan to build savings within the policy; two main types are whole life and universal life; significantly more expensive than term life insurance.

Caveat Emptor: buyer beware.

C.D.: Certificate of Deposit, usually at a bank; savings account with a slightly higher interest rate because of a longer savings commitment (i.e. six months, one year, etc.).

Chapter 7 Bankruptcy: chapter of the Bankruptcy Code providing for liquidation of the debtor's assets in order to repay the creditors; certain assets or aggregate value of assets of the debtor may be exempt based on state law.

Chapter 11 Bankruptcy: reorganization bankruptcy, usually involving a corporation or partnership; generally includes a plan of reorganization to keep a business alive and pay creditors over time.

Chapter 13 Bankruptcy: chapter of the Bankruptcy Code providing for an individual to repay debts over time, usually three to five years; debtor makes periodic payments to the bankruptcy trustee, who in turn pays the creditors; sometimes includes adjustments to debt balances within the bankruptcy.

Checking Account: account set up to maintain daily financial activities. Users can draft checks for payment, issue deposits into their accounts, and keep track of their debit card transactions through their checking account.

Claim: paperwork filed with an insurance company in order to get them to cover a loss.

Co-Insurance: in a health insurance policy, after you pay the deductible the insurance company pays a percentage and you pay a percentage; 80/20 –insurance pays 80% and you pay 20%.

Collision: portion of auto insurance that covers losses due to vehicle damage in an accident.

Commission: a fee paid for providing a service

Commodities: a food, metal, or fixed physical substance that investors buy or sell, usually via future contracts.

Compensation: the total wage or salary and benefits that an employee receives.

Compound Interest: interest paid on interest previously earned; credited daily, monthly, quarterly, semi-annually or annually on both principal and previously credited interest.

Comprehensive: pays for damage to your car that is not a result of an accident.

Consignment Shop: retail store where people sell items and the owner of the shop gets a percentage of the sale.

Consumer: person who buys and/or uses a product.

Contact Letter: a letter informing a prospective employer that you are interested in working for their company.

Contents Insurance: insurance policy that covers personal possessions in a home or apartment.

Conventional Loan: mortgage obtained through the Federal National Mortgage Association (FNMA), which insures against default; generally includes a down payment of 5-20% or more.

Copay: in regards to health insurance, paying a set amount per medical visit.

Cover Letter: similar to a contact letter but is used to inform the prospective employer of your interest and capabilities as they relate to a specific employment opportunity; always accompanied by a resume.

Coverage: applies to the amount of protection you have through an insurance company in the event of a loss.

Cosigning: offering to guarantee someone else's loan; becoming responsible for loan repayment if the borrower defaults.

Credit: money owed.

Credit Bureau: an agency which collects the credit history of consumers so that creditors can make decisions about granting loans.

Credit Card: tool used to finance a purchase.

Credit Disability: insurance that pays for financed items or purchases if you become disabled and are unable to earn an income.

Credit Laws:

- **Fair Credit Reporting Act (1971):** federal law governing the reporting of debt repayment information; establishes when a credit reporting agency may provide a report to someone; states that obsolete information must be taken off (seven to 10 years); gives consumers the right to know what is in their credit report; requires that both a credit bureau and information provider (i.e. department store) have an obligation to correct wrong information; gives consumers the right to dispute inaccurate information and add a 100-word statement to their report to explain accurate negative information; gives consumers the right to know what credit bureau provided the report when they are turned down for credit.

- **Fair Credit Billing Act (1975):** federal law that covers credit card billing problems and applies to all open-end credit accounts (i.e. credit cards and overdraft checking); states that consumers should send a written billing error notice to the creditor within 60 days (after receipt of first bill containing an error), which the creditor must acknowledge in 30 days; requires the creditor to investigate and prohibits them from damaging a consumer's credit rating while a dispute is pending.

- **Fair Debt Collection Practices Act (1978):** federal law that prohibits debt collectors from engaging in unfair, deceptive, or abusive practices when collecting debts; requires collectors to send a written notice stating the name of the creditor and the amount owed; prohibits contacting the consumer if he or she disputes the debt in writing within 30 days (unless collector furnishes proof of the debt); requires collectors to identify themselves on the phone and limits calls to between 8:00 a.m. and 9:00 p.m. unless the consumer agrees to another time; prohibits calling the consumer at work if requested.

- **Equal Credit Opportunity Act (1975):** federal law that ensures consumers are given an equal chance to receive credit; prohibits discrimination on the basis of gender, race, marital status, religion, national origin, age or receipt of public assistance; prohibits lenders from asking about plans to have children, or refusing to consider consistently received alimony or child support payments as income; grants the consumer legal rights to know why he or she was denied credit.

- **Truth in Lending Act (1969):** federal law that mandates disclosure of information about the cost of credit; mandates that the finance charge (i.e. all charges to borrow money, including interest) and the annual percentage rate (APR) must be displayed prominently on forms and statements used by creditors; provides criminal penalties for willful violators, as well as civil remedies; protects against unauthorized use of one's credit card, limiting personal loss to $50 if the card is lost or stolen.

- **Fair Credit and Charge Card Disclosure Act (1989):** portion of the Truth in Lending Act that mandates a section on credit card applications that describes key features and cost (i.e. APR, grace period for purchases, minimum finance charge, balance calculation method, annual fees, transaction fees for cash advances, and penalty fees such as over-the-limit fees and late payment fees).

Credit Life: insurance that pays for financed items or purchases in the event of your death.

Credit Report: report showing your payment history.

Credit Union: not-for-profit cooperatives of members with some type of common bond (i.e., employer) that provide a wide array of financial services, often at a lower cost than banks.

Curb Appeal: the appearance of a home from the street.

Currency: money.

Custodian: one who is responsible for an account listed in someone else's name.

D

Day Trading: establishing and liquidating the same position or positions within one day's trading.

Debit Card: type of card, often bearing the seal of a major credit card company, issued by a bank and used to make purchases; unlike a credit card, the money comes directly out of a checking account; also called check card.

Debt Consolidation: act of combining all debts into one monthly payment, typically extending the terms and the length of time required to repay the debt.

Debt Snowball: preferred method of debt repayment; includes a list of all debts organized from smallest to largest balance; minimum payments are made to all debts except for the smallest, which is attacked with the largest possible payments.

Deductible: amount you have to pay out-of-pocket for expenses before the insurance company will begin to cover all or a portion of the remaining costs.

Deduction: an amount subtracted from something especially as an allowance against tax.

Deed: the legal document conveying title to a property.

Deflation: a broad, overall drop in the price of goods and services; the opposite of inflation.

Delinquency: broadly refers to not being current on your payments.

Depreciation: a decline in the value of property; the opposite of appreciation.

Direct Deposit Service: a service that electronically transfers all or part of any recurring payment, including dividends, paychecks, pensions and Social Security payments directly to a shareholder's account.

Direct Transfer: movement of tax-deferred retirement plan money from one qualified plan or custodian to another; results in no immediate tax liabilities or penalties, but requires IRS reporting.

Disability Insurance: policy that insures a worker in the event of an occupational mishap resulting in disability; compensates the injured worker for lost pay.

DISC Personality Profile: a behavior profile test that yields insights into how you process decisions and what your natural tendencies may be.

Discipline: self control used in directing behavior; the key to wealth building is being consistent over time.

Discount Points: used in the mortgage industry in reference to government loans, meaning FHA and VA loans. Discount points refer to any "points" paid in addition to the one percent loan origination fee. A "point" is one percent of the loan amount.

Disposable Income: amount of money left over after all necessities and expenses are paid.

Dividend Distribution: payment of income to mutual fund shareholders from interest or dividends generated by the fund's investments.

Diversification: to spread around one's investment dollars among several different classes of financial assets and among the securities of many issuers; results in lowered risk.

Dividend: distribution of a portion of a company's earnings, decided by the board of directors, to a class of its shareholders; generally distributed in the form of cash or stock.

Down Payment: the part of the purchase price of a property that the buyer pays in cash and does not finance with a mortgage.

Duplicate Checks: type of checks that make duplicate copies as you write them out.

E

Earned Income: payment received for work, such as wages, salaries, commissions and tips.

Educational Savings Account (ESA): after-tax college fund that grows tax-free for educational uses; eligibility based on parents' annual income.

Elimination Period: amount of time that lapses after a disabling event before the insurance company begins to pay benefits.

Emergency Fund: three to six months of expenses in readily available cash to be used only in the event of an emergency; Baby Step 3.

Employee Benefit: something of value that an employee receives in addition to a wage or salary. Examples include health insurance, disability insurance, discounted childcare, etc.

Employer-Sponsored Retirement Savings Program: Tax deferred savings plans offered by employers that provide a federal tax deduction, tax-deferral of contributions and earnings, and in some cases employer matching. They include 401(k) plans for corporate employees, 403(b) plans for employees of schools and non-profit organizations, and Section 457 plans for state and local government employees.

Empowerment: to gain strength emotionally or spiritually.

Entrepreneur: a person who starts a business.

Envelope System: series of envelopes, divided into pre-determined categories, used to store cash for planned monthly expenses; self-imposed discipline tool to assist people in managing their monthly finances; possible categories include food, entertainment, gas, etc.

Equity: the value of a piece of property over and above any mortgage or liabilities related to it.

Estate Sale: type of yard sales with more items, usually the entire contents of a household.

Exchange Privilege: the right to exchange shares in one fund for shares in another fund within the same fund family; typically at no charge or for a nominal fee.

Excise Tax: a tax levied on the purchase of certain non-essential consumer goods such as tobacco, airline tickets, etc.

Expense: the cost of goods or services.

Expense Ratio: the percentage of a fund's average net assets used to pay annual fund expenses. The expense ratio takes into account management fees, administrative fees, and any 12b-1 marketing fees.

Extended Replacement Cost: part of homeowner's insurance policy that pays a percentage beyond the insured price of the home for purposes of rebuilding it in the event of a catastrophic loss. If you do not update this, it will not cover the appreciation of your home (e.g. house is insured for $200,000, but the value goes up to $300,000, you are covered for the $200,000 plus whatever the coverage states).

F

Federal Deposit Insurance Corporation (FDIC): a federal institution that insures bank deposits.

Federal Housing Administration (FHA): federally sponsored agency chartered in 1934 whose stock is currently owned by savings institutions across the United States. The agency buys residential mortgages that meet certain requirements, sells these mortgages in packages, and insures the lenders against loss.

Federal Insurance Contributions Act (FICA): government legislations that funds Social Security.

Federal Reserve System: the monetary authority of the United States, established in 1913, and governed by the Federal Reserve Board located in Washington D.C. The system includes 12 Federal Reserve Banks and is authorized to regulate monetary policy as well as to supervise Federal Reserve member banks, bank holding companies, international operations of US banks, and US operations of foreign banks.

Fee Table: a table, placed near the front of a mutual fund's prospectus, disclosing and illustrating the expenses and fees a shareholder will incur.

Financial Goals: short-, immediate-, and long-term goals that require money and guide a person's future plans and savings decisions.

Financial Plan: a plan of action that allows a person to meet not only the immediate needs but also their long-term goals.

Financial Resources: financial assets that can be accessed when necessary.

Financing: to buy an item with credit; paying over time.

Finite: having a beginning and an end.

Fiscal: having to do with money.

Fiscal Year: accounting period covering 12 consecutive months over which a company determines earnings and profits. The fiscal year serves as a period of reference for the company and does not necessarily correspond to the calendar year.

Fixed Annuity: type of annuity that guarantees a certain rate of return; see annuity.

Fixed Income Securities: investments, such as bonds, which provide current income from a fixed schedule of interest payments. While the level of income offered by these securities is predetermined and usually stable, their market value may fluctuate.

Fixed Rate: an interest rate that does not change over time.

Floor Plan: the basic layout of a home.

Forbearance: agreement of a lender to suspend foreclosure proceedings and allow a debtor to "catch up" a past due account over a specified period of time; lender grants a postponement of loan payments for a set period of time, giving the borrower time to make up for overdue payments.

Foreclosure: process by which the holder of a mortgage sells the property of a homeowner who has not made interest and/or principal payments on time as stipulated in the mortgage contract.

Fraud: a seller's intentional deception of a buyer, which is illegal.

Free Spirit: a person who thinks, "everything will work out fine," and typically hates to deal with numbers.

Front-End Load: sales commission that is paid up-front when shares of a mutual fund are purchased.

Fund Family: a group of mutual funds sponsored by the same organization, often offering exchange privileges between funds and combined account statements for multiple funds.

Futures: a term used to designate all contracts covering the sale of financial instruments or physical commodities for future delivery on a commodity exchange.

G

Garnishment: court-ordered attachment that allows a lender to take monies owed directly from a borrower's paycheck; only allowed as part of a court judgment.

Grace Period: time period during which a borrower can pay the full balance of credit due with no finance charges.

Gratuity: an amount paid beyond what is required usually to express satisfaction with service quality; also known as a tip.

Gross Income: A person's total income prior to withholdings and deductions.

Gross National Product (GNP): measures an economy's total income. It is equal to Gross Domestic Product, plus the income abroad accruing to domestic residents, minus income generated in domestic market accruing to non-residents.

Growth and Income Mutual Fund: fund that buys stocks in larger, more established companies, medium-sized companies or growth stocks; also called a large-cap fund.

Growth Stock Mutual Fund: fund that buys stock in medium-sized companies that have experienced some growth and are still expanding; also called a mid-cap fund.

Guaranteed Renewable: if you have a 20-year policy, the insurance has to provide coverage after 20 years regardless of health; it will only be more expensive because you are older.

Guaranteed Replacement Cost: part of homeowner's insurance policy that pays for the full cost of replacing damaged property without a deduction for depreciation and without a dollar limit.

H

Health Insurance: covers you in the event of illness or injury.

Health Savings Account (HSA): a health insurance plan for self-employed people containing a large deductible. Money saved in this account grows tax deferred. It can be used for medical care with no penalties and no taxes, and may be kept if unused.

Home Equity Loan (HEL): credit line offered by mortgage lenders that allows a homeowner to borrow money against the equity in their home.

Home Inspector: an individual who inspects homes for defects prior to the closing of a home sale to protect the buyer or lender's investment.

Home Warranty: an agreement that ensures the structural soundness of a home.

Homeowner's Insurance: policy that covers a loss due to damage, theft, or injury within one's home.

House Poor: a condition of having a disproportionately high house payment that limits one's ability to maintain the home and/or meet necessities.

I

Impulse Purchase: to buy an item without thinking about it.

Income: earnings from work or investment.

Income Fund: a mutual fund that invests in bonds and stocks with higher than average dividends.

Income Risk: the possibility that income from a mutual fund or other investment will decline either as a fund's assets are reinvested or when a fixed income investment matures and is replaced with a lower-yielding investment.

Income Tax: a progressive tax on the financial income of individuals, companies, deceased estates, and certain bankrupt estates paid to the government.

Index: a statistical benchmark designed to reflect changes in financial markets or the economy. In investing, indexes are used to measure changes in segments of the stock and bond markets and as standards against which fund managers and investors can measure the performance of their investment portfolios.

Index Fund: a mutual fund that seeks to match the performance of a predetermined market benchmark or index.

Individual Retirement Arrangement (IRA): tax-deferred arrangement for individuals with earned income and their non-income-producing spouses; growth is not taxed until money is withdrawn; contributions to an IRA are often tax-deductible.

Inflation: rate at which the general level of prices for goods and services rise.

Inflation Hedge: an asset rising in value, which helps one to keep up with the rising cost of inflation. Real estate can be a great inflation hedge.

Integrity: having to do with a person's honesty and moral attributes.

Interest: 1) charge for borrowed money generally defined as a percentage. 2) money paid to savers and investors by financial institutions, governments, or corporations for the use of their money (such as a 2% return on money held in a savings account).

Interest Only Loan: a mortgage where you only pay the interest.

Interest Rate: percentage paid to a lender for the use of borrowed money.

Interest Rate Risk: the risk that a security or mutual fund will decline in price because of changes in market interest rates.

Internal Revenue Service (IRS): federal agency responsible for the collection of federal taxes, including personal and corporate, Social Security, and excise and gift taxes.

International Stock Mutual Fund: mutual fund that contains international or overseas companies.

Investing: the process of setting money aside to increase wealth over time, and accumulate funds for long-term financial goals such as retirement.

Investment: account or arrangement in which one would put their money for long-term growth; should not be withdrawn for a suggested minimum of five years.

Investment Advisor/Manager: the individual who manages a portfolio of investments. Also called a portfolio manager or a money manager.

Investment Objective: a mutual fund's performance goal, such as long-term capital appreciation, high current income, or tax exempt income.

Investors: people investing in securities, such as stocks and bonds, or other investments, to achieve long-term financial goals.

Interview: a meeting between an employer and an applicant; the employer asks the applicant questions to assess whether he or she has the right social skills and intelligence suitable for the workplace.

J

Job: a regular activity performed in exchange for payment, especially as one's trade, occupation, or profession.

L

Land Survey: a survey that shows where one's property lines and easements are.

Large-Cap Fund: funds comprised of large, well-established companies.

Lease: a long-term rental agreement, and a form of secured long-term debt.

Level Term: this means you pay the same amount for the entire term of the policy.

Liability Insurance: policy that protects an individual in the event of a lawsuit due to injury on one's personal property or as the result of an automobile accident.

Life Insurance: type of insurance designed to replace income lost due to death; traditionally two types: term and cash value.

Liquidity: quality of an asset that permits it to be converted quickly into cash without loss of value; availability of money; when there is more liquidity, there is typically less return.

Loan: temporary borrowing of a sum of money.

Load Fund: mutual fund that sells shares with a sales charge of typically 2-6% of the net amount sold; some no-load funds also levy distribution fees permitted by Article 12b-1 of the Investment Company Act. These are typically 0.25%; a true no-load fund has no sales charge.

Loan To Value (LTV): value of a property versus the amount borrowed against it; Example: a 70/30 LTV means that the property owner owes 70% of the item's worth and owns 30% of the item's worth.

Long-Term Care Insurance: policy that covers the cost of nursing home or in-home care; recommended for everyone over age 60.

Long Term Coverage: coverage for an extended period of time.

Long Term Disability: disability insurance designed to replace lost income for a period of five years or greater.

Loss: the negative difference between total revenue from a business or investment minus total expense.

Low-Load Fund: mutual fund that charges a sales commission equal to 3% or less of the amount invested.

Lump Sum Savings: saving money specifically for a purchase such as vacations or replacing cars.

M

Management Fee: the fee paid by a mutual fund to its investment advisor.

Market Risk: the possibility that an investment will fall in value due to a general decline in financial markets.

Mark-Up: the difference between the wholesale price and retail price.

Maximum Pay: the amount an insurance company will pay before you are dropped from coverage. With health insurance keep at least a one million dollar maximum pay.

Medicare: federal government program that pays for certain health care expenses for citizens 65 or older; managed by the Social Security Administration.

Mid-Cap Fund: mutual fund containing a group of medium-sized companies that are growing.

Money: currency and coin that are guaranteed as legal tender by the government.

Money Market Fund: mutual fund that seeks to maintain a stable share price and to earn current income by investing in interest-bearing instruments with short-term (usually 90 days or less) maturities.

Money Order: a financial instrument backed by a deposit at a certain firm, such as a bank, that can be easily converted to cash.

Mortgage: loan secured by the collateral of some specified real estate property, which obligates the borrower to make a predetermined series of payments.

Mortgage Life Insurance: insurance policy that pays off the remaining balance of the insured person's mortgage at death.

Motivation: a feeling of enthusiasm, interest, or commitment that makes somebody want to do something.

Multiple Listings Service (MLS): computer program used by realtors to search frequently updated listings of available properties in order to find prospective homes for their clients.

Murphy's Law: anything that can happen will happen.

Mutual Fund: pool of money managed by an investment company and invested in multiple companies, bonds, etc.; offers investors a variety of goals depending on the fund and its investment charter; often used to generate income on a regular basis or to preserve an investor's money; sometimes used to invest in companies that are growing at a rapid pace.

Myth: information that has been passed on but is not true.

N

Need: economic goods and services that are basic for living such as food, clothing, and shelter.

Negotiating: to bargain for a lower price.

Nerd: one who is picky about budgeting and numbers.

Nest Egg: sum of money earmarked for ongoing living expenses at retirement or when employment income otherwise stops.

Net Asset Value (NAV): the market value of a mutual fund's total assets, less its liabilities, divided by the number of outstanding shares.

No-Load Mutual Fund: open-ended investment company whose shares are sold without a sales charge; might include other distribution charges, such as Article 12b-1 fees, but a true no-load fund has neither a sales charge nor a distribution fee.

O

Objective: a goal or plan.

Occupational Disability: type of insurance that provides an income in case the insured becomes unable to perform the job he/she was educated or trained to do.

Opportunity Cost: the true cost of something in terms of what you have to give up to get the item; the benefits you would have received by taking the other action.

Out-of-Pocket: what you have to pay.

Owner Financing: type of home loan in which the existing owner acts as the mortgage holder; payments are made to the owner rather than to a mortgage company or bank.

P

Paradigm: your belief system; the way you see or perceive things.

Patience: the ability to wait or delay an action without becoming upset or annoyed.

Pawn Shop: retail establishment selling items that have been traded as security for a cash loan.

Payroll Deduction: amount subtracted from a paycheck, either by government requirement (mandatory taxes, Social Security, etc.) or at the employee's request (health insurance, retirement plan, etc.).

Permanent Disability: disabilities that are ongoing and are not expected to end.

Policy: describes the type of coverage in an insurance agreement.

Portfolio: a list of your investments.

Portfolio Transaction Costs: the costs associated with buying and selling securities, including commissions on trades, dealer mark-ups on bonds, bid-asking spreads, and any other miscellaneous expenses. These costs are not included in the expense ratio.

Pre-Authorized Checking (PAC): system of automatic payment processing by which bills, deposits, and payments are handled electronically and at regular intervals or on a predetermined schedule.

Pre-Paid Tuition: paying for college ahead of time by accumulating units of tuition.

Pre-Tax Retirement Plan: a type of retirement plan where you put money in before taxes have been taken out, but must pay taxes on the money at the time of withdrawal.

Premium: amount you pay monthly, quarterly, semi-annually or annually to purchase different types of insurance.

Principal: original amount of money invested, excluding any interest or dividends; also called the face value of a loan.

Priority: level of high importance or great urgency.

Private Mortgage Insurance (PMI): policy paid by the mortgage borrower that protects the lender against loss resulting from default on a mortgage loan.

Pro-Active: to have a strong initiative; when one happens "to" things.

Procrastinating: to put off until later; waiting until the last minute.

Profit: the positive difference between total revenue from a business or investment minus total expense.

Pro Rata: debt repayment plan by which the borrower repays each lender a fair percentage of the total debt owed when one cannot make the minimum payments on one's debt.

Prospectus: official document that contains information required by the Securities and Exchange Commission to describe an investment.

R

Rate of Return: return on an investment expressed as a percentage of its cost; also called yield.

Realtor: an intermediary who receives a commission for arranging and facilitating the sale of a property for a buyer or a seller. Also referred to as a Real Estate Broker or an Agent.

Reconcile: to match your bank statement with your checkbook, preferably within 72 hours of receiving the statement.

Redemption Fee: fee charged by some mutual funds for selling (redeeming) shares.

Refunding: sending in proofs of purchase to receive cash back or free gifts.

Reinvestment: use of investment income or dividends to buy additional shares.

Rent: periodic fee for the use of property.

Rental Real Estate: buying real estate to rent out as an investment.

Renter's Insurance: type of insurance that provides coverage for accidents, damages and losses in a rental (apartment or house) or dormitory. Renter's insurance provides coverage for personal belongings and liability that may occur from an accident in the insured home.

Replacement Cost: insurance that pays the actual cost of replacing your home and its contents after a catastrophic event.

Repo Lot: a place where items that have been repossessed are offered for sale.

Restoration Services: part of identity theft insurance that assigns a counselor to clean up the mess made when your identity was stolen.

Résumé: personal and work history used for gaining employment.

Retailer: one who buys a product to re-sell.

Reverse Mortgage: used to release the home equity in a property. The home owner either makes no payments and the interest is added to the lien of the property, or receives monthly payments thereby increasing the debt each month.

Risk: degree of uncertainty of return on an asset; in business, the likelihood of loss or reduced profit.

Risk Return Ratio: relationship of substantial reward in comparison to the amount of risk taken.

Rollover: movement of funds from a tax-deferred retirement plan from one qualified plan or custodian to another; incurs no immediate tax liabilities or penalties, but requires IRS reporting.

Roth IRA: retirement account funded with after-tax dollars that subsequently grows tax free.

Roth 401(k): employer-sponsored retirement savings account that is funded with after-tax dollars and subsequently grows tax free.

Rule of 72: a quick way to calculate the length of time it will take to double a sum of money. Divide 72 by the expected interest rate to determine the number of years (72 divided by 8% = 9 years).

Rule of 78: pre-payment penalty in a financing contract; the portion of a "90-days same-as-cash" agreement that states that the entire loan amount plus the interest accumulated over the first 90 days becomes due immediately.

S

Salary: payment for work, usually calculated in periods of a week or longer. Salary is usually tied to the completion of specific duties over a minimum, but not maximum, number of hours. (See wage.)

Sales Tax: a tax levied on the sales of goods and services. It is collected by the retailer and given to the state.

Saving: the process of setting aside money until a future date instead of spending it today. The goal is to provide for emergencies, short term goals, and investments.

Savings Account: accounts at financial institutions that allow regular deposits and withdrawals. The minimum required deposit, fees charged, and interest rate paid varies among providers.

Savings Bond: certificate representing a debt; Example: U.S. savings bond is a loan to the government in which the government agrees to repay to the bondholder the amount borrowed, with interest; government bonds are issued in face value denominations from $50 to $10,000, with local and state tax-free interest and semi-annually adjusted interest rates.

Savings & Loan Associations (S&Ls): financial institutions that provide loans and interest bearing accounts which are federally insured.

Sector Fund: a mutual fund that invests its shareholders' money in a relatively narrow market sector, e.g. technology, energy, the internet, or banking.

Self Esteem: one's attitude about themselves.

Self-Insured: condition of wealth at which time one no longer needs an outside insurance policy to cover a loss.

Share: piece of ownership in a company or mutual fund.

Short-Term Disability: minimal period of incapacitation; often used to describe an insurance policy that insures one's income for the immediate future following an incapacitating event.

Short Term Policy: insurance policy that only covers a minimal period of time.

Significant Purchase: an amount of money you spend, usually $300 or more, that causes some pain to part with.

Simple Interest: interest credited daily, monthly, quarterly, semi-annually, or annually on principal only, not previously credited interest.

Simple IRA: salary deduction plan for retirement benefits provided by some small companies with fewer than 100 employees.

Simplified Employee Pension Plan (SEPP): pension plan in which both the employee and the employer contribute to an individual retirement account; also available to the self-employed.

Sinking Fund: saving money for a specific purpose to allow interest to work for you rather than against you.

Small-Cap Fund: mutual fund that invests in companies whose market value is less than $1 billion; largely consists of smaller, more volatile companies; also called aggressive growth stock mutual fund.

Social Security: federal government program of transfer payments for retirement, disability, or the loss of income from a parent or guardian; funds come from a tax on income, which is a payroll deduction labeled FICA.

Speculative: purchasing risky investments that present the possibility of large profits, but also pose a higher-than-average possibility of loss.

Stock Markets:

- **National Association of Securities Dealers Automated Quotation System (NASDAQ):** the electronic stock exchange run by the National Association of Securities Dealers for over the counter trading. Established in 1971, it is America's fastest growing stock market and a leader in trading foreign securities and technology shares. The NASDAQ uses market makers who trade for their own account and profit on the spread between bid and ask prices. Although once the province of smaller companies, NASDAQ today is where many leading companies are traded.

- **New York Stock Exchange (NYSE):** the NYSE traces its origins back more that 200 years to the signing of the Buttonwood Agreement by 24 New York City stockbrokers and merchants in 1792. The NYSE utilizes a trading floor for traditional exchanges where buyers and sellers meet directly – that is, brokers representing investors on each side of the transaction come together on a price.

Stocks: securities that represent part ownership or equity in a corporation, wherein each share is a claim on its proportionate stake in the corporation's assets and profits, some of which may be paid out as dividends.

Stop-Loss: total out-of-pocket expense for health insurance; once reached, insurance will pay 100 percent.

T

Take-Home Pay: The amount of money one has available after taxes have been taken out of their pay. Total wage, salary, commissions, and/or bonuses minus payroll deductions.

Tax: a government fee on business and individual income, activities, products, or services.

Tax Credit: an amount that a taxpayer who meets certain criteria can subtract from tax owed.

Tax Deduction: expense that a taxpayer is allowed to deduct from taxable income; examples include money paid as home mortgage interest and charitable donations.

Tax Deductible: the effect of a tax deduction, such as charitable contributions and mortgage interest.

Tax-Deferred Income: dividends, interest, and unrealized capital gains on investments in a qualified account, such as a retirement plan, in which income is not subject to taxation until a withdrawal is made.

Tax Exempt: investments whose earnings are free from tax liability.

Tax Exemptions: amount that a taxpayer who meets certain criteria can subtract from a taxable income; see tax credit and tax deduction.

Tax Favored Dollars: Money that is working for you, either tax-deferred or tax-free, within a retirement plan.

Taxable Income: Income subject to tax; total income adjusted for deductions, exemptions and credits.

Term Insurance: life insurance coverage for a specified period of time.

Timeshare: a form of vacation property ownership where a company sells a small segment of time (usually a week) to a customer. The use and costs of running the property are shared among all of the customers, now owners, who bought into the timeshare.

Time Value of Money: money at the present time is worth more than the same amount in the future.

Title Insurance: coverage that protects a policyholder from future challenges to the title of a property that may result in loss of the property.

Total Return: the change in percentage over a particular period in the value of an investment; including any income from the investment and any change in its market value.

Track Record: the past history of something; with investments, look at the five or ten year record.

Turnover Rate: a measure of a mutual fund's trading activity. Turnover is calculated by taking the lesser of the fund's total purchases or total sales of securities (not counting securities with maturities under one year) and dividing by the average monthly assets. A turnover rate of 50% means that during a year, a fund has sold and replaced securities with a value equal to 50% of the fund's average net assets.

U

Umbrella Liability Insurance: high-limit insurance policy that acts as a protective covering over your home and car insurance against liability caused by an accident.

Underwriter: a firm that buys an issue of securities from a company and resells it to investors. In general, a party that guarantees the proceeds to the firm from a security sale, thereby in effect taking ownership of the securities.

Unearned Income: money received for which no exchange was made, such as a gift.

Uniform Gifts to Minors Act (UGMA): legislation that provides a tax-effective manner of transferring property to minors without the complications of trusts or guardianship restrictions.

Uniform Transfers to Minors Act (UTMA): law similar to the Uniform Gifts to Minors Act (UGMA) that extends the definition of gifts to include real estate, paintings, royalties, and patents.

Universal Life: type of life insurance policy, similar to cash value, but with better projected returns.

Unrealized Capital Gain/Loss: an increase/decrease in the value of a stock or security (mutual fund) that is not "realized" because the security has not yet been sold for a gain or a loss.

V

Veterans Administration (VA) Loan: type of mortgage loan designed to benefit veterans that allows for a true zero-down mortgage; generally more expensive than a conventional mortgage.

Value Fund: mutual fund that emphasizes stocks of companies whose growth prospects are generally regarded as sub-par by the market, resulting in stocks typically priced below average based on such factors as revenue, earnings, book value, and dividends.

Value System: a person's priorities, beliefs, and standards considered important.

Variable Annuity: annuity that has a varying rate of return based on the mutual funds in which one has invested; also see annuity.

Variable Life: type of life insurance that is similar to cash value, but buys into mutual funds to project better returns.

Viatical: contractual arrangement in which a business buys life insurance policies from terminally ill patients for a percentage of the face value.

Vocation: what you do for a living that is your "calling".

Volatility: fluctuations in market value of a mutual fund or other security; the greater a fund's volatility, the wider the fluctuations between high and low prices.

W

W-4: a federal tax form filled out by an employee to indicate the amount that should be withheld from his/her paycheck for taxes.

Wage: payment for work, usually calculated in periods of an hour rather than longer. (see salary)

Walkaway Power: the ability to walk away from a purchase when negotiating.

Wants: desires for economic goods or services not necessary in order to survive.

Wealth: accumulating assets such as money and possessions, often as a result of saving or investing.

Win-Win Deal: a negotiation where both parties benefit.

Withholding: a portion of employee's wages or salary deducted for taxes.

Whole Life Insurance: type of insurance that contains a low-yield savings plan within the insurance policy; more expensive than term life insurance.

Work Ethic: how motivated, loyal and honest you are in your work.

Y

Yield: the annualized rate at which an investment earns income, expressed as a percentage of the investment's current price.

Z

Zero-Based Budget: cash flow plan that assigns an expense to every dollar of one's income, wherein the total income minus the total expenses equals zero.